THE SLEAZE FILE

AND HOW TO CLEAN UP BRITISH POLITICS

THE SLEAZE FILE

AND HOW TO CLEAN UP BRITISH POLITICS

JUDITH COOK

BLOOMSBURY

First published in Great Britain 1995
Bloomsbury Publishing Plc, 2 Soho Square, London W1V 5DE

Copyright © 1995 by Judith Cook

The moral right of the author has been asserted

A CIP catalogue record for this book is
available from the British Library

ISBN 0 7475 2183 2

10 9 8 7 6 5 4 3 2 1

Typeset by Hewer Text Composition Services, Edinburgh
Printed in Great Britain by Clays Ltd, St Ives plc

'The people of England, wearied and stunned by parties and alternately deceived by each, had almost resigned the prerogative of thinking. Even curiosity had expired and a universal langour spread itself over the land. The Opposition was visible no more than as a contest for power, whilst the mass of the nation stood torpidly by as a prize.'

Tom Paine, author of *The Rights of Man*,
writing in December 1792

ACKNOWLEDGEMENTS

I would like to thank most especially Liberal Democrat Co-ordinator Neil Stockley; also Frank Dobson MP, Chris Mullin MP, Kathy Ham and Professor Peter Hennessy of Queen Mary and Westfield College, London, and Peter Wright-Davis, editor of *Voice*. I have also had a great deal of assistance from Labour Research, the West Midlands Health Monitoring Unit, the Association of Community Health Councils for England and Wales, Charter 88, the Audit Commission, the National Audit Office and the *Guardian* library.

CONTENTS

PREFACE

The idea for this book began to germinate in the spring of 1994. At that time, my editor David Reynolds and I wondered if people would know what it was about if we called it *The Sleaze File*. By the early autumn, with the book two-thirds completed, there was no such anxiety. As month followed month, week followed week, we were all engulfed in a tide of sleaze. Scarcely a day seemed to pass without some further revelation of dodgy dealings, sexual adventures by pontificating hypocrites, or political ineptitude.

Sleaze has become a buzz word. Sleaze in national and local government, in finance, in patronage (almost above all in patronage), in gravy-train salaries, in Whitehall and in the NHS. Sleaze, in fact, in almost every aspect of life today. According to political commentator Hugo Young, writing in the *Guardian* just before the 1994 summer recess, 'Sleaze is the sleeping issue. It continues to petrify many ministers in this government . . . they worry a lot in private about the overarching possibility that they are regarded as a government of crooks that Asil Nadir helped to power.'

This is not a book about national corruption on the grand scale. There is no suggestion that we are faced with a similar situation to that presently obtaining in Italy. What we have politically is the insidious blurring of the edges between what is correct and what is not. Most of what is recounted in these pages is not strictly illegal – just doubtful. But it all contributes to the climate of sleaze. By the end of 1994, as the stream of revelations became a flood, the government itself had become so alarmed that a Special Committee under the chairmanship of Mr Justice Nolan was set up to look into current standards in public life. It is unlikely to report, however, before this book goes to press.

The government is right to be worried. I honestly believe that politicians of every hue have no real idea of the contempt in which many of them are now held throughout the country, and it should indeed concern all of them, not just the government. The cosy club of the House of Commons insulates our legislators far too well. As the present administration has been in power for the last fifteen years, the examples given, of necessity, apply very much to what has happened during that long period in office. But it is well to remember that it was Harold Wilson's Labour administration in the 1970s which set up the network of Quangos (albeit without the spending powers of those which now operate) that gave the green light to the present government to follow suit; and that few now would be able to teach Mr Wilson anything about patronage, which he used blatantly, again providing an example which has been happily seized on since. But the Wilson and Callaghan adminstrations passed a long time ago and we are here and now.

Any government which has been in power for as long as the current Conservative regime becomes both arrogant and complacent, no matter what the colour of its politics. But this has now been aggravated by the fact that so much power and influence has been put out to non-elected, unaccountable bodies. The temptation to stuff them with placemen and allow them to cut corners is immense, and the ills are exacerbated by a laissez-faire policy of deregulation. It is a climate which permeates the way almost everything is run: industry, business, finance, local services; it is everywhere.

What I have tried to do in the pages that follow is to provide a snapshot of the present situation by gathering together instances of what has gone wrong: abuses of the political system; the ever-increasing use of patronage; the current lack of accountability in all walks of public life; waste, gravy-train salaries and perks; the differences between public and private morality, and the grey area between what is strictly legal and what is not. To give every possible known example would require a whole series of books. I have not dealt with finance, even though the last years have provided a rich field, from Barlow Clowes through the Bank of Credit and Commerce to the Maxwell Pension Fund. This is not because it is not worth writing about, but because it is a very specialist field. However, the financial scandals have also played their part in bringing about the present climate. In the final chapter I look at various ways that have been suggested by which matters might be improved, while the Postscript consists of material still coming in on the issues which have been raised, right up to the time of going to press.

For a substantial proportion of the material I am deeply indebted to the reports of the House of Commons Public Accounts Committee, which has proved itself an excellent watchdog. All too often its startling findings are either ignored by the media or relegated to a couple of paragraphs at the bottom of an inside page. Unhappily, as with all House Committees, its criticisms are by no means always accepted, nor its recommendations acted upon.

August 1994

Chapter 1

THE IRRESISTIBLE RISE
AND RISE OF THE QUANGO

In the great days of the medieval and Renaissance monarchies a king would have to push his way through a jostle of courtiers, place-seekers and petitioners every time he left his private apartments. Patronage was all, favourites were made at the wave of a hand and could just as quickly be destroyed. Power, office (high or low), access to public funds, all were in the gift of the monarch or, to a lesser extent, the powerful nobility. The sign that time was running out for the Earl of Essex came when Elizabeth I withdrew one of his prime sources of income: the monopoly on the tax on all sweet wine entering the country.

It would be pleasant to be able to look back on all this and think how quaint, how corrupt, how splendid that such things are all behind us in this great democracy of ours. Unfortunately, the powers of patronage now in the hands of government would astound even Henry VIII.

'Quango' is an acronym which stands for Quasi-Autonomous Non-Governmental Organisations. Apparently the word was coined as a joke in the late 1960s by Anthony Barker of Essex University to describe bodies outside the civil service, funded by taxpayers, but in the gift of Ministers. In government circles they prefer the acronym EGOs, Extra-Governmental Organisations. Whitehall has never officially used the word Quango, but it has become the popular way of referring to such bodies.

What is now causing mounting alarm is the rapidity with which

Quangos have replaced elected, or partially elected, bodies, with an unelected, unaccountable bureaucracy. They have become a repository for the place-seeker, the power-hungry, those rewarded for services to a political party, those who will be of use to a political party and can be counted on to carry out ideology to the letter, and those with vested interests. Margaret Thatcher, when she came to power, vowed to reduce their number. Instead there is now one for every 10,000 inhabitants of the UK. The whole system of democratic government is becoming tainted as it moves further and further away from those it is supposed to represent. Not since the days of the rotten boroughs (which we will consider in a later chapter) and the overt buying of privilege has there been such universal and deep-seated distrust and cynicism towards Parliament and the whole political process.

Committees and bodies set up to monitor and oversee public business have a long tradition. Indeed the Board of Trade was formed in 1621 as the Committee of Trade, and throughout the seventeenth and eighteenth centuries there were numerous other such organisations. H. Parris in *Constitutional Bureaucracy* notes that 'the system worked well so long as boards were responsible in fact, as well as in name, to the King. But once the executive became primarily responsible to Parliament, the system came under strain. The result was a decline in the board pattern of administration and its supersession to a large degree by a ministerial pattern.'

Over the years, the number of such bodies rose and fell but were rarely a cause for major concern. It is the last twenty years which have brought them to prominence. The Labour Party in the 1970s was highly criticised for the number and variety of the Quangos it set up. Then, as now, patronage operated in appointments made to such bodies, but today there is at least one major difference. While Labour too used seats on Quangos as a reward for loyalty, political service and to ensure their make-up was politically correct, 1970s Quangos operated almost entirely as advisory bodies and talking shops. They had influence but no major political clout and they had little or no responsibility for spending taxpayers' money.

They were, however, open to criticism. During a House of Commons debate in 1977[1] it was revealed that thirty-nine members of the TUC held some 180 public appointments. Jack Jones, General

Secretary of the Transport and General Workers' Union, held ten such places, on organisations such as the National Economic Development Corporation and the Crown Agents, while a further handful of worthies held twenty-seven posts between them.[2] The situation was spelled out by George Woodcock, former TUC General Secretary, when he described the criteria used to make such appointments: 'Seniority, the muscle power of your union and competence. These are what you need to get a public job and in that order of priority.' In other words, Buggins's turn rules OK. Labour Ministers, and certainly Harold Wilson as Prime Minister, made openly political appointments. A third of the existing Chairmen of Area Health Authorities were replaced with Labour supporters in 1977. Roy Hattersley MP, speaking on BBC Radio's *File on Four* on 7 June 1978, explained why it was necessary to put the right people on Quangos: '. . . having set up such an agency, I would want to believe that I'd so equipped it in terms of the membership that they took the right individual decisions.' This is a message the incoming Conservative government took to heart and has implemented in spades.

The official number of 'Extra-Governmental Organisations' (EGOs) listed in the Cabinet Office publication *Public Bodies* is 1,389, thus 'proving' that the Conservative government, true to Margaret Thatcher's promise, has reduced their number. This is, however, to be economical with the truth. The present administration does not count as Quangos bodies such as the various executive agencies, boards of hospital trusts and so on, even though their members, too, are appointed and they handle public finance; by all previous criteria they would certainly have been described as Quangos. In 1994 Democratic Audit and Charter 88 published *EGO Trip*, the most detailed investigation yet into the number and scope of all bodies officially designated as Quangos and those which fulfil Quango criteria. (Democratic Audit is a project that is enquiring into democracy in the UK. It is sponsored by the Rowntree Trust and based at the Human Rights Centre at Essex University.)

The report shows that the number of Quangos stands, at the time of writing, at 5,521, an astronomical rise and almost four times the number the government is prepared to recognise. Like mushrooms they appear overnight, speeded on their way by pressure on schools and hospitals to opt out of local education and health authority control. Together these unelected, unaccountable people are currently spending the mind-bending sum of £48.1bn a year; that is nearly a third of the entire public spending of the nation and a sum which has risen by 24 per cent in real terms since the Conservatives came to power in 1979. The Quangos vary in size from the boards of school governors and small NHS Trusts, which deal with sums of thousands or tens of thousands, through such disparate bodies as the Scottish Crofters' Board, the Apple and Pear Research Council and the ironically named Westminster Foundation for Democracy to the Training and Enterprise Councils (£2.3bn), Further Education Funding Council (£24.2m) and the District Health Authorities (£11.65m). Unlike councillors they do not even have to inform us of what they intend to do and if we dislike the result or consider them to be either at best incompetent or at worst corrupt, we cannot vote them out of office.

The earlier jokey reference to Henry VIII seems all too apposite as Ministers use their wide-ranging discretionary powers to the uttermost. One method has been the implementation of Statutory Instruments, the systematic use of what are called 'Henry VIII' clauses to direct policy in very wide terms indeed. Henry VIII clauses empower Ministers to issue Statutory Instruments which give them powers to change parliamentary Acts without further legislation. To quote *EGO Trip*: 'These powers are often taken in legislation which is controversial in itself. No comprehensive list of accretion of executive powers exists, but in a single Act, the Education Reform Act of 1988, Jack Straw MP estimated that the Education Secretary took 415 new powers of central control – a figure not challenged by the Minister.' It is, *EGO Trip* continues, the existence of EGOs which makes the adoption and use of powers on this scale possible. Never has there been so much banging on about freedom of choice and devolving power, never for hundreds of years so much centralisation of it.

Quangos were originally defended on the grounds that they stood at arm's length from the government of the day. Not any more. Today's Quangos are unashamedly the creatures of Ministers, enhancing their already alarming powers to ignore both Parliament and public opinion. As the authors of *EGO Trip*, Stuart Weir and Wendy Hall, point out, a prime example of this is the way a Conservative government, barely represented in Scotland and not at all in Wales, can keep a tight control on both countries.

Ministers have total freedom to decide when and where a Quango should be set up. There is no requirement for any consultation as to whether or not it is necessary, its remit or its appointees. Treasury Minister Stephen Dorrell, questioned on this in July 1993, replied that the decision to create an executive agency was determined solely 'by our judgement in each case as to where the long-term interests of taxpayers lie'.

There is no list of the full membership of Quangos in the public domain and the names of appointees can only be discovered with great difficulty. Yet nearly three times as many people serve on these unelected bodies as there are local and county councillors: 70,000 as against 25,000 elected representatives.[3] In 1993 Baroness Denton, then a junior Minister at the Department of Trade and Industry, had personally made over 2,000 appointments and was quoted in the *Independent on Sunday* on 28 March of that year as saying, 'I can't remember knowingly appointing a Labour supporter.' Asked to clarify her statement on *File on Four* on 13 July she said, 'Of course you don't put in people who are in conflict with what you are trying to achieve. It's no good going on an NHS Trust Board if you don't believe in the policy the Department of Health is pursuing.'

The ministerial explanation for appointments is that they have sought to bring in the expertise primarily of business people – a laudable aim, but one which ought to be balanced by those with other interests. However, it appears there is another field of expertise which is warmly welcomed, that of donating funds to the Conservative Party. A major new Quango is the Funding Agency for Schools, a body which may eventually have effective powers over the entire education budget and conduct of the state school system. Of the thirteen government appointments, two have links with companies regularly donating to the Conservative Party. Sir Christopher Benson, the Quango's Chairman, is a former Chairman of a Housing Association, Chairman of the Sun Alliance

Group, which has donated £280,000 to the Tories during the last six years; a director of the MEPC property group, which donated £25,000 to the election campaign in 1992; and Chairman of Costain, which also donates to party funds. His annual salary in post for a two-day week is £33,430.[4] Another member, Stanley Kalms, Chairman of Dixons, also donated £25,000 in 1992. Two other prominent Tory members of the same Quango are Sir Robert Balchin, a regional party Chairman, and Edward Lister, leader of the Tory flagship London Borough of Wandsworth Council. Sir Robert is also Chairman of Grant-Maintained Schools Mutual, an insurance scheme for schools that have opted out of local authority control. This scheme is being underwritten by – Sun Alliance International.[5] For years Sir Robert has been actively encouraging schools to opt out and is quoted as saying, 'John Patten told me that the first criteria for membership of the board was that you must be supportive of the concept of grant-maintained schools.'

Various investigations by the Labour Party and the press have come up with lists of other donators to the Conservatives. A Labour Party paper, *Quangos and Donations to the Tory Party*, reveals thirty-two, appointed to eleven executive bodies, including the Housing Corporation, Scottish Enterprise Board and Welsh Development Agency, and thirteen appointed to six urban development corporations. An investigation by the *Observer* on 4 July 1993 revealed that fourteen Chairmen or Chief Executives of Quangos were involved in businesses which had contributed substantially to Conservative Party funds.

Speaking in a Commons debate on 24 February 1994 on the subject of unelected bodies, Labour's Michael Meacher drew the attention of the House to a possible link between party donations and appointments to Quangos. As well as raising the case of Sir Christopher Benson, he also noted that Neil Clarke was appointed Chairman of British Coal when, as a former Chief Executive of Charter Consolidated, he gave £26,000 to Tory Party funds; that Sir David Nickson, appointed Chairman of the Scottish Enterprise Board, is a director of three companies that contribute to party funds, one of them, Scottish and Newcastle Breweries, handing over £75,000 and another, Hambros, £53,000. Sir Nigel Mobbs, appointed Chairman of the DTI Advisory Panel on Deregulation, is also Chairman of Slough Estates, which gave £44,000 to the Conservatives, and Vice-Chairman of Kingfisher, which donated £25,000.

Michael Meacher went on to point out that the Chairmen of no fewer than twenty Quangos appointed by Conservative Ministers are associated with generous donators. They include the Takeover Panel, the Welsh Development Agency, the Port of London Authority, the London Tourist Board, the Highlands and Islands Enterprise Board, the Top Salaries Review Body and the Medical Research Council. He concluded by suggesting that Quangos were now 'so stuffed' with Tory workers and donators 'that one genuinely wonders whether "Quango" really stands for "Quite Assuredly Now Government Orchestrated".'

To quote Democratic Audit again: 'In the absence of systematic information about public appointments, it is difficult to establish whether such donations make a difference. It is also impossible to inquire into other issues, such as whether certain companies are rewarded for political donations with places on boards that have influence over investment and regulation in the areas where the companies are commercially active. There may or may not be scandals to be uncovered in the distribution of public appointments. It is already a scandal that this should be unknowable.'

Labour MP Alan Milburn, trying to find out who had been appointed to the new National Health Service trusts, found that out of the 185 such appointments he was able to discover, sixty-two had direct links with the Conservative Party. Among these, twenty-two had served as Tory councillors, fourteen had worked for the party, nine had high-level links with companies donating to party funds, eight were former MPs or parliamentary candidates, five were spouses of prominent Conservatives, three were prominent party supporters and one was a Conservative peer. One hundred and seven Chairpersons were currently directors of companies and forty-five retired directors; thirty described themselves as 'consultants', and twenty-seven were in the legal profession, eight having retired from it. Twenty-eight had links with education, twenty-two with accounting and finance, twenty-two were listed as managers, nine as surveyors and eight as either councillors or MPs. On the other hand, only five had current medical links, three worked in local government, two were clergy and there was a single, retired, miner. A mere seven chairs had Labour Party links and just one was connected with the Liberal Democrats.

Party donations and political activity apart, there is growing disquiet about the professional interests of those appointed to Quangos. Stuart Weir has researched medical Quangos in particular and was quoted in the *Observer* (3.7.94) as saying, 'Government is at a great disadvantage in its dealing with transnational corporations. It sets up advisory committees and recruits expert advisers, but two-thirds of the members of five key Quangos we have studied have a huge range of interests in powerful pharmaceutical, chemical and food companies. Nine of the fifteen members of the Committee on Toxicity of Chemicals in Food, Consumer Products and the Environment, have a "consultancy interest" in companies such as Cadbury-Schweppes, SmithKline Beecham, Roche Holdings and Proctor and Gamble.'

Labour MP Peter Kilfoyle, who has asked some 800 parliamentary questions in an attempt to discover the membership of all the government-appointed trusts, advisory committees and funding agencies, says that while there may be no impropriety, 'the public should be aware of these interests in appointees to public bodies. It is vital that the government explains why the powerful drug companies are so well represented on the public bodies that monitor our medicines. The public has a right to know whether their health, or the health of corporate profits, is of greater importance to these Quango members.' Kilfoyle asked William Waldegrave, Minister for, among other things, Open Government, if he would now publish an annual directory of those appointed to public bodies, 'to include the names, addresses, remuneration, period of office and political and pecuniary interests of all those so appointed'. The short answer was no.

According to Kilfoyle, William Waldegrave wrote to him saying that there was little or no public interest in Quangos. It is a pity that information on what can happen in an atmosphere of secrecy and patronage does not hit the headlines more often, although examples grow by the week.

A recent one which did make the press was that of Tory Party member Anne-Marie Nelson. Ms Nelson was obviously considered to be of such tremendous value that she was unlawfully appointed to the Chairmanship of two health trusts, thus receiving two salaries. Ms Nelson is also busy elsewhere, serving on a training Quango in Kent. The Secretary of State for Health, Virginia Bottomley, personally invited Ms Nelson to chair both the West Kent Health District and the Special Hospitals Service Authority (SHSA). Prior to her appointment to West Kent, Ms Nelson had chaired the Maidstone Health District from 1982 to 1994 at a fee of £17,145. An additional sum of £15,855, from the SHSA, which runs Broadmoor, Rampton and Ashworth special security hospitals, brought her earnings from these posts to £33,000.[6]

At first the Department of Health seemed set to brazen it out, but finally admitted that the second appointment had been unlawful under the Regional and District Health Authorities Members and Procedure Regulations of 1990. Indeed, junior Health Minister Dr Brian Mawhinney had stated in a Commons written reply only the previous February that 'Chairmen and non-executive members of NHS authorities may not serve concurrently on more than one such authority'.

Virginia Bottomley was thus forced into making an apology. 'I regret,' she said, 'the mistake that was made over her appointment to the SHSA. Obviously Ms Nelson herself was in no way at fault over this and I have conveyed to her my own and the department's apologies for the difficulty and embarrassment that has been caused.

'Though regrettable, this was an honest mistake by the department which arose from the worthwhile objective of strengthening the links between the special hospitals and the NHS. This is something to which Mrs Nelson has already made an important contribution.'

The Department of Health swiftly announced that any decisions taken under Ms Nelson's chairmanship would stand, as the 1977 NHS Act states that an authority's proceedings would not be invalidated by 'any defect in a member's appointment'. Nor would Ms Nelson be asked to pay back any of her £15,855-a-year fee for chairing the SHSA, since she had put in 'many hours' work in good faith'.[7]

However two NHS Quangos, the NHS Supplies Authority and

the National Blood Authority, set up in April 1993, were, for some unknown reason, exempted from the 1990 Procedure Regulations and the affair of Ms Nelson shone a spotlight on the case of Sir Robin Buchanan, who resigned as Chairman of the Wessex Regional Health Authority in August 1993 following revelations of computer contract losses by the authority to the tune of £63m. Virginia Bottomley had allowed him to keep another part-time health Quango chair, that of the NHS Supplies Authority, at a salary of £21,000. Asked about the dual role of Sir Robin, ex-Tory Councillor and close friend of Chris Patten, now Governor of Hong Kong, a Department of Health spokesperson said, 'We will look into this matter when the time comes to review the regulations.'

The NHS Supplies Authority, with its staff of 4,500, is the largest purchasing organisation in Europe and accounts for £1.7bn of NHS spending. In the summer of 1993 NHS trust chiefs accused it of wasting £100m a year through mismanagement. According to a confidential survey of 145 NHS trust Chairmen and Chief Executives, leaked to the *Observer*, this authority is still offering a substandard service.

In Wales, which has hardly any Conservative MPs, there has long been speculation as to how appointments to Quangos are made and what criteria are used. As well as political affiliations, it has also been suggested that a good route to such a post is by way of being able to give 'a funny handshake'.[8]

In June 1993 the House of Commons Committee of Public Accounts published one of its most damning critiques ever, that of the Welsh Development Agency's accounts for 1991–92.[9] The WDA is Wales's biggest and most prestigious Quango. First came criticism of losses of £1.4m incurred on redundancy payments where agency members were unaware of the government's expectation that, as members of a local government pension scheme, they should adopt local government terms. This, said the committee, was made clear in the WDA Act of 1975 and 'we regard it as quite unsatisfactory that the Agency did not consult the Welsh Office on this important matter'.

Then there was the question of one of the perks the WDA had awarded itself, about which the committee took a dim view. 'We consider it unacceptable that the Agency should have provided cars to their Board members and senior executives without requiring them to pay for private motoring.' The board was further criticised for 'the breakdown in financial controls' which led to their incurring £33,000 of irregular expenditure on their car scheme. 'We note that, in 1984, the Agency decided that senior officials should no longer be required to meet the petrol costs of their private mileage and that the then Chairman and Chief Executive were under the impression that the Agency had sufficient power to make these changes. We find it hard to understand why the Agency were unaware of the clear requirements to obtain the approval of the Welsh Office for such a change.'

The committee also considered that the employment of a 'Mr Carigman, a United States citizen, to lead their inward investment operations in North America' was unsatisfactory, not least because of the said Mr Carigman's totally 'inadequate knowledge of Wales', and the fact that because of the agency's 'inadequate and contractual supervisory arrangements' Mr Carigman had been able to remove and sell furniture bought with WDA money at a cost of £53,288. 'We do not consider that the agreement under which Mr Carigman will repay the Agency $15,000 for this furniture and equipment represents good value for money.'

Even stronger criticism was levelled at the board of the WDA over the appointment of a Mr Neil Smith and 'for allowing his bogus credentials to pass unchecked before his appointment as Director of Marketing'. Mr Smith's references were not taken up, which was unfortunate, as it later transpired that he had a criminal record and had previously been in trouble when working for a Trafalgar House company called Sight and Sound Education. Among other activities, Mr Smith paid out public money to the Shapes Model Agency and had eleven girls from the agency sent up to his hotel room for interview to see if they were suitable for advertising promotion.

Then there was the golden handshake of £233,000 paid out to an employee after a long period of what the then Chief Executive, Philip Head, described to the committee as 'gardening leave'.

The committee then turned the spotlight on the WDA's Chairman, Dr Gwyn Jones, who resigned, along with Philip Head, shortly after the report's publication. Dr Jones was closely questioned about why he had not notified the first change of use of the premises for which he had received a Rural Conversion grant, and why there had been a ten months' delay before the agency decided that the change was not material and a clawback not applicable. 'It is clearly important that persons in high public office should ensure that circumstances do not arise which can give cause to any allegations of abuse of position. We consider therefore that Dr Jones should have notified both of the proposed changes in use at the earliest possible opportunity.'

Of Dr Jones, it concludes, 'Regarding Dr Jones's appointment as the Agency's chairman, we note that no references were sought before the Secretary of State appointed him to this post. We also note that he was subsequently given a number of other public and private appointments, some of which may well have resulted from his Chairmanship of the WDA. We consider it important that references should be sought before the initial appointment to senior posts in the public sector of persons with no, or limited, experience of the financial and other disciplines expected in the public sector.' Dr Jones had, in fact, been appointed to the boards of a number of other Quangos – the Welsh Water Enterprise Board, the BT Wales Advisory Board – and, on 1 January 1992, he was appointed BBC National Governor for Wales on the direct recommendation of the then Home Secretary and the Secretary for Wales. By convention, this latter appointment carries with it membership of the authority of S4C, the Welsh equivalent of Channel 4, and the Home Secretary duly appointed Dr Jones to it on the same date. At the time of writing he is still in post.

The committee reserved its final blast for 'Operation Wizard', the progress of which was neither formally minuted by the board nor its existence publicly revealed. Operation Wizard was set up to examine various privatisation possibilities, and financial and accounting consultants Touche Ross, Barclays de Zoette Wedd and Outram Cullinan were engaged on a consultation basis to advise on the feasibility of restructuring and possible privatisation of parts of the agency. Professional fees relating to this probject totalled £308,000 of public money, spread over the years 1988–91. The costs were charged in such a way that they could not be separately identified as relating to Operation Wizard. The committee's report concludes: 'Whilst we recognise there was no breach of Government accounting, we are concerned that there might have been a deliberate attempt by the Agency to conceal Operation Wizard within their accounts by spreading the costs under several headings. We do not believe this to have been compatible with Parliamentary accountability, especially as some of the options identified by the consultants involved major restructuring of the Agency, with changes to its objectives and the possible reduction of its specific commitment to Wales. We are concerned that not only was Parliament denied information but that this Committee would have remained unaware of the project's existence had it not been for unofficial revelations from within the Agency.'

Among those questioned by the Public Accounts Committee was the Welsh Permanent Secretary Sir Richard Lloyd Jones. At the end of this hearing Labour MP Alan Williams said to him, 'You have listened as we have listened to what the WDA have said today. I must say that what has come over to me is their incredible arrogance, lack of contrition and almost smugness. Have you been alarmed at what you have heard? Would you, for example, leave here a happy man if you thought that all the Quangos in Wales were behaving as the WDA has behaved?' Sir Richard replied that he would leave a happy man from what he knew 'of much of the WDA's management'.

On 5 May 1994 the BBC current affairs programme *Week in Week Out* claimed that the government used the WDA to pump more than £7m into areas of the country with marginal Conservative constituencies, in spite of a warning from lawyers that such activity was illegal and outside the Quango's remit. A spokesman for the Welsh Office said that while there might have been 'a technical breach of funding', it would have been 'cumbersome to have done it any other way. The allegation that there was a political [motive for channelling funds to these particular areas] is baseless'.

Naturally there is no room here to give details of all 5,521 Quangos, but Democratic Audit lists over fifty for Wales and substantially more for Scotland. Those connected with the Department of Education, such as the Further Education Funding Council (£24.2m), Schools Examination and Assessment Board (£23.3m) and the National Curriculum Council (£8.5m), handle vast amounts of public money, as do the Quangos associated with the Departments of Employment, the Environment and Health.

Eighty-six per cent of Quangos are exempt from scrutiny by any Ombudsmen. While parents might complain to an Ombudsman about schools run by local authorities or about council housing, there is no such recourse to outside assistance in the case of the 2,668 housing associations, the 1,025 grant-maintained schools, the 577 colleges of further education or the 164 universities.

Only 33 per cent of Quangos have their finances scrutinised by the Audit Commission or the National Audit Office. No Quango has to release any of its policy papers to the public, as local elected councils do. In February 1994 the boards of four grant-maintained schools in Essex decided, as a matter of policy, to restructure local education, thus creating 'élite' schools. Even that Tory diehard Teddy Taylor said this would be 'massively damaging to able, working-class children'. Ninety-nine per cent of parents voted against the plan but, as Sir Teddy told the House, 'It was explained that parents were entitled only to consultation. The boards are going ahead with their proposal and are presenting their plan to the Secretary of State for Education.'

Members of Quangos can make unlimited errors of judgement, massive and financially damaging mistakes and decisions of doubtful probity. Yet there is no redress. Unlike elected councillors and council officials, they cannot be surcharged and found personally liable for, for example, 'wasting public money'. Unlike most EEC countries, Britain has no single statute governing the conduct of Quangos and few provisions by which the public can demand consultation, disclosure of information or a legal remedy for bad decisions.

Democratic Audit notes that not since the Crichel Down affair in 1954 have Ministers of either party shown an inclination to accept responsibility for the mistakes or bad judgement of their own departments.

The Crichel Down affair is very apposite to the present situation with regard to ministerial responsibility. Briefly, in 1939 the Air Ministry bought up land from three farms in the Crichel Down area of Dorset for use as a bombing range. By 1949 the land was no longer needed and the original owners asked if they could have it back. They were refused. They then offered first to buy it back and second to rent it, but again they were refused. A large sum of public money was then spent putting the land right, rebuilding farm buildings, etc., before the whole was turned over to the Crown Commissioners, who promptly let it to what is described in the subsequent report as 'a favoured tenant', who had no previous connection with the area.

The original owners demanded, and finally got, a Public Inquiry, chaired by Sir Andrew Clark QC. His report, published in June 1954, found no evidence of financial corruption, but said that there had been substantial improprieties and a variety of errors. Sir Andrew also noted that there had been a 'regrettable attitude of hostility' towards the original owners, 'engendered by a feeling of irritation that any member of the public should have the temerity to oppose, or even question, the acts of public officials'. However, the then Conservative Agriculture Minister, Sir Thomas Dugdale, still saw no reason to change the original decision and refused to take any further action. There followed first a stormy meeting with his own backbenchers, then the announcement of a debate, which was subsequently delayed. When it finally took place, on 20 July 1954, it was noisy and bad-tempered. Sir Thomas was supported in his stance by his Labour predecessor, Tom Williams MP, who had been responsible for the original decision.

Sir Thomas made every possible excuse, from blaming his actions on bad advice from his officials to claiming that he was only implementing the existing policy of his predecessor. However, he was finally forced to resign on the grounds of 'the principle of ministerial responsibility' for what had occured.[10]

But the logical outcome of current reforms, the disabling of local government and the proliferation of Extra-Governmental Organisations, is to make Ministers virtually the single ultimate point of responsibility for the billions of spending and policy decisions of the host of 5,521 Quangos, ninety-four 'executive agencies' and 439 local authorities. A very modern ideology has produced a practical nonsense equivalent to medieval calculations of the number of angels capable of dancing upon the point of a pin.

The irresistible rise and rise of the Quango raises the executive, as Democratic Audit notes, 'above the judiciary and Parliament and institutionalises its independence from Parliamentary scrutiny and accountability.

'The spread of EGOs (Quangos) is a symptom of a systemic disease. The body politic itself has to be cured if they are to be brought under democratic control.'

Chapter 2

JOBS FOR
THE BOYS AND GIRLS

Many of the chapter subjects in this book overlap since patronage appointments cover all those who have been selected by government Ministers or departments for a wide range of posts, some of which are with Quangos and some of which are not. It would be possible to fill this book with examples, but in the interests of space, a handful must suffice to show how prevalent it now is for people with little or no relevant experience to be appointed to well-paid jobs, and for them to remain in post despite evidence of inefficiency or corruption.

The Welsh Connection

Following the criticism of the Welsh Development Agency, the Welsh Office has now published the names of appointees to all 'recognised' bodies and it is at once apparent that there has been no halt to the flow of patronage in the principality.

For instance, Brian Thomas, now on the Countryside Commission for Wales 'gained valuable experience for this public post' as chauffeur to the then Welsh Secretary, David Hunt, during the 1992 election.[1] Indeed, gratitude for the stout work done at that difficult time was obviously of help when it came to selecting a new Chairman for the Welsh Development Agency, the post being given to the person who had helped frame the Conservatives' appeal to expatriate voters.

When Jonathan Evans left the Board of Housing for Wales to take his seat in the House of Commons, also in 1992, his place was taken by a Tory candidate who had not been so fortunate. The current head of the Welsh Conservative Party has been made Chair of the Welsh Consumer Council, and a former Tory Party candidate has recently been appointed Chair of the Higher Education Funding Council for Wales.

Keeping on Track

The summer of 1994 was one of discontent on the railways with a succession of strikes by signalmen. The signalmen had long been promised a pay review, following increases in productivity coupled with considerable job losses. The vital importance of reliable signalling equipment and top quality operatives was emphasised in the various investigations into the 1988 Clapham Junction railway disaster in which thirty-three people were killed and two hundred injured. Few would deny that signalmen daily hold the lives of thousands of people in their hands – quite a responsibility.

1994 also saw the fragmentation of British Rail in the run-up to privatisation. A new body, Railtrack, was to be responsible for the track and signalling, 'selling' its services to what may well be a multiplicity of users once the franchises are awarded for different parts of the network.

The government decided to appoint Robert Horton as Chairman of Railtrack and he duly took up his post in April 1994. Horton is not only a government supporter, he also has a reputation for taking draconian decisions. During his time as a senior executive for BP he sold off half the company's tanker fleet and laid off 60 per cent of the work force. However, he would not, he says, describe himself 'as a train buff'. When 'ousted', as the *Guardian* describes it, from his position as Chairman of BP, he received a pay-off of £1.5m. His salary then was £787,000 per annum. On 8 July 1994 Transport Minister Roger Freeman revealed that Mr Horton was being paid £121,800 a year as Chairman of Railtrack for a three-day week.

The subject had arisen when it was discovered that two men with strong links with the Conservative Party had just been appointed to the Railtrack board. They are engineer Sir William Francis and a Mr William Wilson, whose background is in financial services. Both will serve as non-executive directors. Sir William was Vice-Chairman of the construction company Tarmac from 1974 to 1977 and a director of Trafalgar House from 1978 to 1986. Both companies have been regular contributors to Tory Party funds. He is also a former Chairman of the West Midlands branch of the Conservative Party.[2]

Mr Wilson is a non-executive director of the Royal Bank of Scotland, whose Chairman is George Younger, former Tory Defence Secretary. It is with this bank that the Conservatives currently hold their overdraft.

The matter initially came to light when Labour's Shadow Transport spokesman, Frank Dobson, wrote to Roger Freeman, asking what other fringe benefits and bonuses Railtrack board members received apart from their part-time salaries. 'The answer,' he says, 'revealed not only old "Spanish Customs" but new Spanish customs arranged as a perk for board members.

'The answer makes clear that part-time members of the Railtrack board, in addition to their £10,000 salary, get a £500 bonus every time they actually turn up to do any work.' They are paid out of our – the taxpayers' – money. Labour and Liberal Democrat MPs were quick to compare this remuneration with Horton's dismissal of the claim to bonuses and allowances being made by signal staff. Derek Fatchett, Labour's rail spokesman, pointed out that these payments were more than three times the signal staff's basic weekly wage.

Roger Freeman also conceded that Railtrack's Chief Executive, John Edmunds, receives £131,950; Norman Broadhurst, the Finance Director, £150,000; David Moss, the Commerical Director, £100,000; and David Rayner, Director of Safety Standards, £90,000.[3]

Looking after Group 4

During 1993 much wry merriment was caused by the activities of the firm awarded the government contract for transporting prisoners from prison to court or prison to prison. In the teeth of opposition from both prison staff and police, the Home Office had gone ahead with this piece of privatisation and awarded the contract to the security firm Group 4. Group 4 operates out of a remote headquarters near the Cotswolds village of Broadway and keeps itself to itself.

The merriment was caused by the number of prisoners lost during the early weeks of the experiment, although the laughter faded after a prisoner drank himself to death with vodka while being transported around the country by Group 4. After the contract had been awarded it was discovered that Conservative Party Chairman, Norman Fowler MP, was one of Group 4's directors. He later resigned, after weeks of protesting that this personal interest had no bearing on the fact that the contract had been awarded to that particular security firm.

Nor was that the only link between those in high places and Group 4. In June 1994 the Public Accounts Committee disclosed that Group 4 had been awarded a contract to run a prison by a senior civil servant who later joined the company; the award was made in spite of the fact that Group 4's bid for the Wolds Prison on Humberside was higher than two rival tenders and that more than £1.5m in hidden extras had been paid to the company.

Enquiries made by the *Observer* revealed that Group 4 made £500,000 in its first year of running the Wolds, which had opened in April 1992. By 1993 profits had fallen to £195,000. The drop was alleged to have occurred because during the first year the company had economised on both staff training and prison facilities.

On 19 June 1994 the *Observer* published a further example of possible conflict of interest: that a senior Home Office adviser to the excellent Chief Inspector of Prisons, Judge Stephen Tumin, had been receiving consultancy payments from Group 4's private prisons' subsidiary company. David Jenkin joined the Prisons' Inspectorate as a research consultant to the Chief Inspector in

1987. He has since, according to the press report, worked a thirty-six-hour week at the inspectorate, while continuing to carry out his research for Group 4. He had visited the Wolds on inspectorate business and been involved in discussions of the judge's report on it one year before his involvement with Group 4 began.

The knowledge of Mr Jenkin's Group 4 consultancy has even caused concern within the Home Office itself. An unnamed senior governor told the *Observer*, 'It is totally inappropriate for a senior adviser to the Chief Inspector of Prisons to be paid by one of the companies he inspects.' In reply Mr Jenkin said he did not see himself as a civil servant: 'My contract manager treats me as an independent firm. In return I provide research services on prison regimes. Because I am an independent consultant I am free to take on other work on a commercial basis. Every arrangement I make is with the knowledge of the Home Office. A conflict of interest has never arisen. I value the independence of the inspectorate very highly.'

Group 4 stated that the company had to 'buy' expertise which was only available from the Home Office and Prison Service. They saw nothing improper in the arrangement they had with Mr Jenkin.

A Non-Partisan Organisation

In April 1994 it was announced in a written parliamentary answer that Mr Andrew Turner had been appointed Chief Executive of the new Grant-Maintained Schools Foundation. This Quango, the Department of Education has assured critics, is a non-partisan organisation set up entirely to advise schools on whether or not they should opt out of local education authority control.[4]

At that time Mr Turner was pretty busy. He was an Oxford

City Councillor and was standing as the Conservative candidate for East Birmingham in the forthcoming European elections. He had also hit the headlines early in 1994 during the notoriety surrounding Tim Yeo, MP for Suffolk Central, and his liaison with Miss Julia Stent, which will be dealt with in more detail in Chapter 10. Mr Turner was a former boyfriend of Miss Stent and it was gleefully reported in the tabloids that it was he who had introduced Miss Stent to Mr Yeo at the 1992 Conservative Party Conference.

Andrew Turner has long been a vocal supporter of schools opting out, but this did not prevent his appointment to the 'non-partisan' foundation. The foundation receives £500,000 of public money and so far the bulk of the information it has provided is in favour of opting out. It has been impossible to discover what Mr Turner is paid for his position on this Quango, although Westminster sources put it at about £50,000 per annum. Labour MP Stephen Byers, whose parliamentary question revealed the appointment in the first place, then wrote to Sir John Bourn, Auditor and Comptroller General, demanding an investigation into how it had been made and whether or not there had been open competition for the post.

The new foundation was established after critical reports from Commons committees about the 'entanglement' of government funding for the Grant-Maintained Schools Centre, which provided services for opted-out schools, and an organisation headed by Mr Turner called Choice in Education, devoted to campaigning for schools to opt out. According to the *Guardian* (21.4.94), the two organisations shared an office and the centre received a government grant of no less than £790,000 in 1993. The line of the Department of Education and Education Ministers is that there is no official funding to campaign for opting out, and they have regularly attacked local authorities and parents' organisations which have funded campaigns against it. Choice in Education was hurriedly wound up when it was revealed that Mr Turner's salary was being paid by the Grant-Maintained Schools Centre, which claimed this was done 'for administrative convenience'.

Among other directors appointed to the foundation are Sir Robert Balchin, knighted for his work for grant-maintained schools, and Lawrie Norcross, an activist for the Tory think tank Institute for Policy Studies. Asked by the *Guardian* for a comment, a Department of Education spokesman said, 'Mr Turner was appointed by the directors of the foundation. It is nothing to do with us.'

Country Matters

In spite of government reassurances, there is much public concern over the problems caused by the cattle disease known as BSE and whether or not there is a biological route by which it can affect human beings. The whole matter boiled up again in the spring of 1994 when Germany threatened to ban all beef imports from this country. The government's line has always been that BSE cannot pass into humans and that they have this on the best possible independent advice.

In July 1994, announcing the preliminary results of an experiment to trace the biological routes through which BSE develops in cattle, Agriculture Minister Gillian Shepherd told the House, 'My Right Honourable Friend the Secretary of State for Health and I have sought the advice of the Spongiform Encephalopathy Advisory Committee (SEAC) and have considered this with the Chief Medical Officer.'

In a letter to the *Guardian* (8.7.94), the persistent Peter Kilfoyle, Labour MP for Walton, pointed out that SEAC is yet another Quango, as is the Meat and Livestock Commission which handles exports. He had had to spend a considerable amount of time prising the names of SEAC members out of the government and apart from the names, he could find out little or nothing about their credentials or abilities. SEAC, he writes, is jointly funded by MAFF (Ministry of Agriculture, Fisheries and Food) and the Department of Health at a net cost in 1992–93 of £500,000. It publishes no annual report. Its Chairman receives £162 a meeting – a paltry sum compared to that paid to those sitting on the Railtrack Quango. Its board consists of five male members and one female, who each receive

£130 a meeting. It is not required to publish any of its advice to government, so there is no way of knowing the premises on which that advice is based.

Mr Kilfoyle contrasts this with another Quango, the Committee on Carcinogenicity of Chemicals in Food and Consumer Products, which is charged with assessing and advising on the toxic risk to humans of substances such as additives in food. It does produce an annual report and for the first time its members have been made to declare their commercial interests. Five of its thirteen members declared a consultancy interest in some seventeen companies; two were shareholders in six companies; two were employees of major pharmaceutical or food companies; and one was currently receiving a grant and another a pension from a company in which they had a commerical interest.

The companies included the Wellcome Foundation, SmithKline Beecham, Roche Holdings, Proctor and Gamble, the tobacco giant BAT, and the International Sweeteners Association. In March Mr Kilfoyle had written to William Waldegrave, the 'Minister for Open Government', asking him yet again if he would publish a directory of all those appointed to public bodies. As ever, he replied, 'No.' Mr Kilfoyle continues, 'I would argue that the public would be very interested to know the names of the people who are appointed by Ministers to supply them with advice on the safety of the food and drugs they consume.

'It is right that the public should know that the powerful drug companies are so well represented on the public bodies that monitor our medicines. They, and indeed red-blooded, beef-eating Food Ministers, have a right to know if the food industry is similarly represented on SEAC.'

Turning up the Gas

A cross between Boudicca and Annie Oakley is how the *Guardian* described Clare Spottiswoode, the recently appointed Director General of the gas consumers' watchdog, Ofgas. In November

1993 she replaced Sir James McKinnon, who was that rare creature, a true consumers' watchdog who had made himself deeply unpopular in some circles owing to the frequent battles he had had with British Gas in an effort to make them keep their prices down.

Ms Spottiswoode, appointed by the President of the Board of Trade, Michael Heseltine, at once went for a high public profile and was prolix in personal details of her life, from her schooling at Cheltenham Ladies' College, her switch from Maths to Economics while at Cambridge, where she took part in bed races and achieved an Upper Second, to her happy home life and weekend domestic bliss at the family's Suffolk cottage.

Unlike her predecessor, Sir James, she was soon on the best of terms with the Chief Executive of British Gas, Cedric Brown. According to Mr Brown she achieved more in eight days than her predecessor had in eight years. Her tabloid reputation as Boudicca came from the way she used her close links with the DTI to demand the publication of a consultation paper which, it was thought, might well lead to the putting up of gas prices in tens of thousands of homes. This has since been proved to be a correct assumption. The general opinion was that she appeared to be putting the interests of the gas industry before those of the consumer.[5]

In May 1994 Michael Heseltine and John Gummer, Secretary of State for the Environment, were forced into ordering an inquiry into the way Ms Spottiswoode had been appointed to her £70,000-a-year post, following allegations that she had compromised the independence of Ofgas through too close a relationship with the DTI and British Gas. Sir Peter Gregson, Permanent Secretary at the DTI, was asked to investigate her relationship with civil servants. The move came about after the Conservative Chairman of the Commons' Environment Committee told Ministers that its members were challenging her competence after what they had described as 'an appalling performance' before the committee the previous March, when, according to the view expressed by the committee, she had appeared totally unprepared to answer the questions they put to her and had compounded this by attacking her predecessor, Sir James McKinnon.

MPs had two particular complaints. One was Ms Spottiswoode's use of former Conservative Minister Sir Peter Morrison, who had also been Parliamentary Private Secretary to Mrs Thatcher, as a consultant whose advice she had taken on how to handle evidence to the committee. Of even more concern was the part John Michell, the Under-Secretary for Oil and Gas at the DTI, may or may not have played in her appointment. The committee had been told that her name had not been included in the original list recommended by a firm of outside head-hunters, but had been added later by Mr Michell, who also took a prominent role in recommending her for the post. After her appointment, Ms Spottiswoode had sent Mr Michel two dozen red roses and he later accompanied her on a trip to Brussels and on a visit to Canada to look at the role of gas regulators. Both trips were at public expense.

During a further grilling by the committee in May, Ms Spottiswoode was questioned over her decision to curb a £125m-a-year subsidy to help cut energy bills for the disabled and pensioners, something which had been actively promoted by her predecessor. At the earlier hearing, she had alleged that Sir James had acted illegally in funding energy initiatives, an allegation which had deeply offended Sir James, who later appeared before the same committee to prove the legality of his action. He told the committee that Ms Spottiswoode's allegation had left him feeling his reputation had been 'besmirched'.

On 25 May 1994 Ms Spottiswoode again appeared before the committee, which pointed out that Sir James had acted properly and legally; she then withdrew her allegation. She was also warned by the Conservative Chairman, Robert Jones, about comments made to the press by her husband. Because of the allegations concerning the part played by Mr Michell in her appointment, this hearing was broadened to cover both her appointment and her relationship with private policy advisers. Ms Spottiswoode told the committee that she had been approached by head-hunters who thought her 'an ideal candidate' and that she had worked in the Treasury at the same time as Mr Michell, who was going to interview her. 'When I saw him,' she told them, 'I recognised him, but he did not recognise me.'[6] After a brief investigation into the matter, Sir

Peter Gregson reported back that there had been no conflict of interest with regard to Ms Spottiswoode's appointment.

Development by Moonlight

'Government planning adviser moonlights for developers' ran a headline on 25 April 1994. The story, picked up by several newspapers, pointed out that the government's chief planning adviser, David Lock, was also a paid consultant to the very development companies which were trying to override the green-belt policies of the Department of the Environment. Professor Lock, appointed to his post in January 1994, is paid £28,000 per annum for a two-and-a-half-day week, which enables him to continue to appear at public inquiries on behalf of developers opposing the Department's planning guidelines.

In February Professor Lock was the advocate for Landmatch, a Hertfordshire company, at a planning inquiry in South Bedfordshire. After purchasing the land at £2,000 per acre, Landmatch was seeking to have it redesignated. Professor Lock told the inquiry that the 145 acres at Hockliffe, right on the A5 trunk road, should be changed from farmland to building land. Such a redesignation would be likely to produce a multi-million pound profit. At the time of writing a decision is still awaited.

Objectors at the inquiry noted that Landmatch contributed to Conservative Party funds in the two years up to its 1993 annual report, but when questioned by the *Guardian* (25.4.94), its Managing Director, Nicholas Woolley, said the company had since ceased making such donations. The busy Professor Lock also appeared at the same inquiry on behalf of Blue Circle Cement, who wish to develop a business park at the Houghton Regis quarry, part of a Site of Special Scientific Interest.

Asked about a possible conflict of interest, a Department of Environment spokeswoman, who confirmed that Professor Lock also had a third job, that of Visiting Professor of Town Planning at the University of Central England in Birmingham, told the *Guardian* that the professor always declared an interest in projects in which he had a personal involvement outside his departmental duties. He had notified them of his work for Landmatch. 'The department is aware of all his work.'

Professor Lock set out his views on the need for new developments in South-East England in a pamphlet entitled *Riding the Tiger*, published in 1989. Its foreword notes that the views expressed 'challenged the long-established orthodoxy of green belts'.

Scrapping the Ban

On 9 June 1994 Roads Minister Steve Norris admitted in a written reply to the Labour MP Glenda Jackson that donors to the Conservative Party were among those lobbyists who had persuaded the government to scrap the London lorry ban. Among them was one of the biggest corporate donors, United Biscuits, which in 1992 had given £130,000 to party funds, the largest single donation that year. Its 1993 annual report showed that it gave £40,000. Directors of two other companies which contribute to the party were also instrumental in the drawing up of proposals to scrap the ban.

It was further revealed that the Chairman of the Transport Deregulation Task Force was Duncan Black, also Chairman of John Swire and Sons, which donated £221,000 to the Conservative Party in 1993; another member of the task force was Graham Millar, Operations Director of Youngers plc, which donated £413,000 to Conservative funds.

Among ten other companies listed as lobbying for the ban to be withdrawn was Sainsburys, in which Trade and Industry Minister Tim Sainsbury has a significant interest. While there is no suggestion that this fact was not known, it might be thought that there might be a conflict of interest as he was then the Minister in charge of guiding the Deregulation Bill through the Commons.

Political Advice

In April 1994, following a series of questions from the Liberal Democrat MPs Archie Kirkwood and Matthew Taylor, the government stood accused of handing out 'nice little earners to party hacks'.

The questions concerned the number and cost of political advisers. In a written reply to Archie Kirkwood, the Prime Minister, John Major, said there were some forty-one currently in post. About a third had been recruited directly from Conservative Central Office. The list, which includes a note of their previous employment, shows advisers drawn from, among other organisations, Coopers and Lybrand, the *Daily* and *Sunday Telegraphs*, the University of California, the Shopping Hours Reform Council, stockbrokers James Capel, Hanson plc, Haymarket Publishing Services Ltd (President of the Board of Trade Michael Heseltine's company), Namara Cowan, English Estates and the Conservative think tank the Public Policy Unit.[7]

Some advisers, it transpires, earn more than the Prime Minister himself, the highest earner (unnamed) reaching £100,080 against Mr Major's £76,234. Between them the advisers cost the taxpayer £1.4m a year, double the amount set aside for this purpose in 1988. No information was given as to who earned what, apart from the fact that salaries were below £20,000 for junior staff, fourteen were in the £40,000–£60,000 band, three in the £80,000-plus band and one earning £100,000.

Asked by Matthew Taylor what procedures were in place to ensure that special advisers attached to Ministers had no pecuniary or other interests that might conflict with their duties,[8] John Major replied, 'Special advisers are subject to the same rules on conflict of interest as other civil servants ... Advisers are allowed more freedom of political activity than other civil servants to the extent that, with the approval of their Minister, they may attend party functions, including party conference, may maintain contacts with party members and may take part in policy reviews conducted by the party.'[9]

In response Matthew Taylor complained that the structure amounted to a fast-track career for young Tory high-fliers, who could move straight from Central Office to government and then sell their expertise to the private sector. 'Why should they bother to go to the trouble of getting elected when this route is so attractive?' It was, he said, a lucrative career for former Tory hacks.

Whenever the question of patronage arises, the present government insists that neither party membership nor political donations have any bearing on appointments, which are made strictly on the basis of merit. Yet all the statistics collected by a wide range of bodies show that a substantial proportion of those appointed to Quangos, executive agencies, etc, do have such connections or belong or have belonged to organisations which have donated funds. That there is genuine cause for concern is shown by the fact that this is an area which now comes within the remit of the Nolan Committee.

Chapter 3

RIVERS OF GOLD –
POLITICAL FUNDING

On 14 April 1994 the House of Commons Home Affairs Committee published a report with the title *The Funding of Political Parties*. The need for the committee to deliberate on the subject followed a number of disclosures during the run-up to the 1992 general election. These had included the fact that the Conservative Party had received two substantial tranches of funding, one from a Greek shipping tycoon, John Latsis, and the other from a prominent Hong Kong businessman, Y. K. Po. In 1993 came the investigation into the affairs of the Cyprus businessman Asil Nadir, during which it came to light that he had illegally given £440,000 to the party. On numerous occasions both inside the House and out of it, the then Conservative Party Chairman Sir Norman Fowler was asked why he did not return this money once it became known that the donation had been illegal. So far this has not been done.

However, amid growing concern over the identity of political paymasters and what they expected to get in return, it was decided that the Home Affairs Committee should look into the whole question and recommend whether or not there should be substantial changes in the way funding was handled.

Sir Norman himself gave evidence to the committee and made it clear from the outset that he saw no reason to change a system he felt was working extremely well: donations to political parties should be kept secret if that was what donor and recipient preferred. The public did not need to know who was funding whom and why. Asked if he thought the fairest way and one open to least abuse was for the state to fund all legitimate political parties, Sir Norman saw no necessity for it whatsoever. An element of humour came into the proceedings when, questioned specifically about the donations from Messrs Latsis and Y. K. Po, Sir Norman replied diplomatically that Mr Y. K. Po 'is now dead'. 'He wasn't when he signed the cheque,' retorted Labour MP Chris Mullin.

When it came to writing up its conclusion, the Conservative majority on the Home Affairs Committee agreed with everything Sir Norman had had to say, seeing no need for anything other than a little tinkering at the edges. No case had been made for the publication of the names of substantial donors and there was certainly none for the state funding of political parties. The main body of the report positively oozes complacency:

'The financial integrity of British public life is still, thankfully, such that a requirement of this kind is not necessary. We see no reason why parties which have little public support should be either financially dependent on the taxpayer or be able unjustifiably to undermine the income of those who enjoy that support.

'In a free society which cherishes the secret ballot we believe that it would be wrong to oblige the disclosure of commitment to a political party by a requirement to identify financial benefactors.' Nor, they continued, should there ever be any ceiling on what a party could spend during an election campaign, thus preserving the imbalance by which the Conservative Party is regularly able to spend far in excess of any other. So, in the best of all possible funding worlds, everything is for the best. Or is it?

So incensed was the Labour minority on the committee by the conclusions of their colleagues that they published their own, sepa-rate, Minority Report which was presented by Chris Mullin. (For convenience this will be referred to as the Minority Report from now on.) The committee chairman, Sir Ivan Lawrence, backed by the Conservative majority, had, it seems, voted down attempts by Labour to call for questioning Lord McAlpine, Conservative Party Treasurer throughout the 1980s, and Sir Bryan Wyldbore-Smith, who ran the party's fund-raising. Labour members were also denied a trip to North Cyprus to question Asil Nadir further about the illegal donation of £440,000, despite the fact that he had stated publicly that it had been given partly in the hope of his getting a knighthood.[1]

The view of Labour, the Liberal Democrats and of the smaller parties is that all donations over a certain amount should be publicly acknowledged. The preferred sum would appear to be £5,000. This is not some revolutionary or outlandish new notion. It would not be thought controversial in the United States, Canada, or most EEC countries. The Minority Report points out that there is only one party, the Conservatives, which opposes such openness in Britain and that there are even some Tories who believe their party should be more open about its financial affairs.

Labour, as is well known, receives its most substantial funding from the trade unions, although this has obviously diminished considerably as unemployment has risen and union membership fallen away. However, it can usually rely on the unions donating substantial sums when it comes to a general election. The Liberal Democrats, on the other hand, have to manage as best they can without any such safety net, and it is to their credit that they have achieved so high a profile on so little finance. Other parties scrabble for pounds as best they can.

Because of the discrepancy in funding, particularly the amount the Conservatives are able to spend on general elections and all the secrecy surrounding the donations it receives, various investigators have made it their business over the years to try to discover who is funding the Conservative Party. What follows is based on the findings of the minority group on the Home Affairs Committee and some excellent work by the *Independent* and Labour Research. The latter, which is neither funded by nor affiliated to the Labour Party, publishes a monthly magazine and a number of reports, largely aimed at the trade unions.

The General Position on Funding

'The funding of the Conservative Party is one of the great mysteries of British politics,' states the Minority Report. 'No one, least of all the Conservatives, knows where most of the party's money comes from. It has been estimated that in the four-year period from April 1987 to March 1991 the Conservative Party received £37.9m in Central Office donations, of which £21.9m cannot be traced to any source from any published record. Such sources as have been identified have come not from information published by the Party but from painstaking work by assiduous journalists, organisations such as Labour Research (no relation to the Labour Party) and, in the case of Mr Asil Nadir, for example, as a result of criminal or civil proceedings.'

Central Office accounts for the year ending March 1992, which covered the run-up to the general election, showed a total income of £23.5m, which included constituency donations of £1.3m and others of £20m. Of this latter, Labour Research has managed to trace the source of only £4m.

On the other hand, the Labour Party's total income for 1992 was £16.6m, of which £8.5m came from trade union affiliation fees, £1.6m from membership subscriptions and £4.9m from fund-raising. The amounts given by each union are available for inspection from the audited and published accounts of the unions concerned, and the party made available to the committee details of the twelve biggest donors. In oral evidence before the committee, Labour Party General Secretary Larry Whitty said that individual donors included fifteen people who gave over £10,000 before the election campaign and that in future the Labour Party would publish the source of such donations irrespective of what the Home Affairs Committee might decide. Mr Whitty defined a 'substantial donation' as in the region of £5,000.

The Liberal Democrats' total income for the 1992 election year was just over £3m. Thirty-five per cent came from membership subscriptions and 61 per cent from donations. Most donations were small and Mr Timothy Razall, the Party Treasurer, told the committee that this was because 'we do not have people with large money bags to write out cheques for us'. He did not wish to give the names of larger donors, although he said that the party would be quite willing to publish this information in the future, should the Home Affairs Committee decide that the rules should be changed. Labour Research, sifting through corporate donations for 1992, found that only two of the accounts they examined disclosed donations to the Liberal Party: Marks and Spencers (£10,000) and the hotels group Buckingham International (£2,000). In 1983 the old Liberal Party had received a one-off donation of £183,000 from the British School of Motoring. Regarding overseas donations, Mr Razall saw no reason to turn these away so long as the source was properly disclosed.

Of the other parties, the Greens said the largest donation they had ever received was £100,000 and recommended disclosure of all individual donations over £5,000. Plaid Cymru believed that 'controls should be placed over the sources of finance of political parties' and the Scottish National Party favoured disclosure of any donation over £20,000. The Ulster Unionists provided accounts disclosing a central income of £116,000, only £1,280 of which came from donations. It is clear from all this, therefore, that when it comes to political funding the Conservatives have a major advantage.

Of particular interest to the minority members of the Home Affairs committee was a memorandum from Mr Eric Chalker, who, between 1989 and 1993, represented the Greater London area on the Conservative Board of Finance, the body which theoretically oversees the financial affairs of the party. He was also Joint Treasurer. Mr Chalker wrote, 'There is no higher body with financial responsibility within the Party on which a place can be secured by direct election . . . yet members of the Board are consistently denied more than the barest minimum financial information.'

He told the committee[2] that when he had first joined the board its members did not even receive copies of the annual income and expenditure accounts, 'which Central Office have published, with great reluctance, since 1984'. There is still no formal presentation of these figures to the board and its approval is not required. He had been elected, he continued, 'with a specific mandate to pursue the quest for more information than had previously been available. As a consequence I regularly sought details of Conservative Central Office expenditure, I regularly sought examination of their budgets and I regularly sought some discussion of what was clearly (to me, at least) an impending financial crisis. It was all virtually to no avail. The paid employees and the vested interests obdurately stood their ground and democratic accountability was non-existent.' Board members were actually *entitled* to some of the information he had sought by virtue of the board's constitution, but it was made clear to him that board members – despite having been elected – were effectively there as guests of the unelected board Chairman, in whose hands power lay.

Of his four years on the board, Mr Chalker said, 'Over £67m of expenditure was recorded by Central Office in that time, but nobody had to account for one penny of it to the Conservative Board of Finance or any other elected body.' During his period of office more than £43m had been donated, most of its origins being kept from board members. Following press reports in 1991 of large secret donations, he had asked the Chairman for information which would reassure him and his constituency party as to their source. He wanted to know if there was any limit to the amount of finance the party would accept from any one donor; whether or not any donor had ever been turned away or any donation declined; and whether there was any established policy which would prevent acceptance of a particular donation or would subject one that was offered to careful scrutiny. He never received any reply.

Searching for the Rivers

Not only are the sources of donations to Conservative Party funds not made public, over the years those in charge of finance have been prepared to go to the most elaborate lengths to conceal their origins. In 1989 the *Independent*, by means of internal documents which had come into its hands, revealed an intricate system of conduits for cash and the purpose of a number of front organisations.[3]

For the first time light was shone on a series of companies whose existence had hitherto only been rumoured. These are the 'River' companies, hidden channels for corporate cash donations. They were set up way back in 1949 by no less a person than Sir Winston

Churchill, then Leader of the Opposition. They were called River companies not because of their purpose as cash channels, but because they were named after British rivers. There were originally eight of them, using rivers whose names began with the letters A to H. Five were dissolved in 1984, leaving, at the time of the *Independent*'s investigation, those called after the Rivers Arun, Bourne and Colne. In 1989 the directors and shareholders included Lord McAlpine and Sir Oulton Wade (both party treasurers) and the previously mentioned Sir Bryan Wyldbore-Smith, Director of the Conservative Board of Finance. At the time of the publication of the Home Affairs Committe report, Chris Mullin noted that so far as the committee could ascertain, these three companies still existed.[4]

According to the *Independent* (16.1.89), only sketchy details of their activities were available at that time at Companies House because the River companies did not have to file records until 1968 and the limited accounts filed after that did not reveal the source of their income. But the paper held evidence that the companies received almost £2.6m income from UK companies between 1954 and 1963, well over a third of the Conservatives' £6.2m income from donations in this period.

Other money conduits included British United Industrialists (BUI), and the Northern Industrial Protection Association. In some cases the system was made even more complicated by the channelling of funds first to BUI, who then passed them on to the River companies, who finally passed the sums on again to Conservative Central Office. One marvels at the need for so secret and Byzantine a system.

BUI was founded in 1948 by the first Lord Renwick to fight nationalisation and 'preserve, protect and promote the interests of free enterprise'. Between 1949 and 1980, almost £10m was channelled from companies through BUI to the Conservative Party. In a letter soliciting donations from businessmen before the 1987 general election, BUI's Director General, Alastair Forbes, confirmed, in Chris Mullin's view, that its purpose was to disguise political donations from shareholders. He wrote, 'We believe that a donation to BUI is less emotive than a donation to the Conservative Party appearing as a note in your financial statements.'[5]

In a promotional leaflet published at the same time, Ian Weston-Smith, BUI's Chairman, wrote, 'Prior to 1980 there was always a basic understanding that some companies shrink away from any form of publicity in this domain and derive much comfort from the knowledge that, if they so wish, the 1967 Companies Act only requires them to record under political donations "BUI £x".' BUI was a useful channel 'for arm's length encouragement and financial support for the anti-militant sector of the trades union movement' and 'a face acceptable to Scottish Industrialists'.[6]

Among the hundreds of companies which, according to the *Independent*, have used BUI over the years are Marks and Spencer (£226,000) and Reckitt and Colman (£400,000).

About 90 per cent of money sent to BUI was passed on to Central Office, the rest going towards other organisations it supported such as the Economic League, which maintains a blacklist of so-called leftwingers and subversives, and Aims of Industry, which ran a series of anti-Labour advertisements during the 1987 general election campaign.

In 1989 the *Independent* noted that by that time BUI had ceased to use the River companies and instead passed on its donations to the Drummonds Bank Free Enterprise Account, a party bank account not mentioned in the limited information published by Central Office. According to its promotional leaflets, BUI, as it was an unincorporated association, had never had to file any documents at Companies House.

Lord Taylor, President of the major construction company Taylor Woodrow, was questioned by the paper as to why BUI was set up. He replied that the desire for secrecy among industrialists was paramount throughout the period from 1954 to 1979, regardless of which party was in office. His own company had donated £30,000 to BUI the previous year, had altogether given some £174,800 between 1954 and 1979 and had also contributed directly to the Conservative Party. He claimed to know nothing of the role of the River companies.

The aim of businessmen, he said, had been to provide the Conservatives with the resources to fight Labour, while hiding the fact from 'militant shop stewards and Labour Councils responsible for the award of commercial contracts'. Union leaders, he declared, 'would not hesitate to call strikes against employers found to be Conservative supporters and some Labour Councils adopted a vicious attitude in awarding contracts. The Conservative Party needed funds very badly and the industrialists were frightened of their name being displayed as supporting the Conservatives.'

They did not want a party that would use nationalisation to rob industry and close the grammar schools, but many industrialists had fought shy of declaring these beliefs, which was why BUI had been set up. Lord Taylor himself had seen the organisation as a way of keeping up the pressure on successive Tory administrations to keep 'on the straight and narrow path' of free enterprise. 'We had to fight Harold Macmillan to stop him going socialist,' he claimed, 'and, but for Aims of Industry, Edward Heath would have agreed to putting trade union leaders on the boards of companies.'

He concluded by saying that more companies were contributing directly to the party in 1989 because of the 'unique leadership of Margaret Thatcher'. There was less sense of urgency, since many industrialists now felt that the Conservatives would remain in power for ever. According to the Minority Report, BUI ceased to exist some time after the last general election.

Offshore Companies and Foreign Friends

In a letter to *The Times* on 29 June 1993, Mr John Strafford, a member of the Conservative Board of Finance from 1989 to 1992, wrote, 'Everyone is now clear that the Conservative Party uses off-shore accounts . . . I know from my own experience that a large amount of funds raised on behalf of the Conservative Party goes into accounts which are not in the name of the party. This applies not only overseas but to accounts in the UK.' On 17 June 1993 Lord McAlpine told ITN News that the party had 'tons of off-shore accounts'. On 26 June 1993 the *Independent* revealed that Mr Octav Botner, once head of Nissan UK, had channelled large donations to the party through an off-shore bank account in Jersey. Sources close to Botner informed the paper that this idea had been suggested by senior Tory Party officials. He had begun by trying to get a clutch of Tory MPs to sit on his board and when this had not proved possible 'he hit on the idea of donating to the party as a way of acquiring influence'. Like Mr Nadir, Mr Botner is currently wanted in the UK by the authorities, in his case regarding allegations of involvement in a huge tax fraud. Also like Mr Nadir, he is now abroad. He denies that he is a fugitive from justice, claiming that he is residing in Switzerland due to health problems. The illegality regarding Asil Nadir's donations was that the payments were made on company cheques, but were not disclosed in the company accounts. The Minority Report makes it clear that because members were unable to call various witnesses for questioning, it was impossible to determine the extent of off-shore funds.

During the committee's deliberations, Labour Party spokesman Frank Dobson drew attention to an issue he felt had received relatively little publicity. Through a series of written parliamentary questions he had established that between 1988 and 1991 fourteen government Ministers had visited Hong Kong on public business and, at the expense of taxpayers, had spent some of their time there engaged in party political activity which included fund-raising.[7] Those involved included John Major and Foreign Secretary Douglas Hurd. Dobson had felt that most people of all political persuasions would find it unacceptable that Ministers of the Crown, 'whose fares and accommodation are paid for by the taxpayer should, while abroad on public business, take time off to raise funds for their party'.

British tax laws are generous to foreign businessmen. Unlike his counterpart in the USA, where global income has to be declared for tax purposes, a businessman living in Britain who claims his main home is overseas is not liable for UK tax on income earned abroad. In 1991 John Major hosted a dinner at 10 Downing Street for wealthy Asian businessmen, ten of whom had this special dispensation. According to one of the guests, Mr Sarosh Zaiwalla, interviewed on the Thames Television programme *This Week* on 5 March 1992, there had been some discussion as to whether or not this loophole might be closed. 'The Prime Minister did say he had considered this when he was Chancellor, and because of the representation which was received from the City, especially from the Greek community, it was not considered suitable to bring in the domicile amendment.'

According to the *Financial Times* (24.11.93), Mr Major's fund-raising Downing Street dinners have been resumed, although he had said that he no longer wished to continue with the dinners. 'The occasions have been kept secret because of acute sensitivity about the party's finances in the wake of the political row over donations from Mr Asil Nadir, the fugitive businessman.' An *Evening Standard* report of the same date says, 'This represents a climb down by Mr Major who had set his face against blatant fund-raising in Downing Street after the political embarrassment caused by Tory Party links with Asil Nadir.' It went on to quote an unnamed party fund-raiser who said that 'the goodwill generated by a Downing Street dinner can lead to a donation of up to £20,000 a head. A dinner for twenty could raise up to £400,000.'

Company Matters

The stark contrast between the secrecy surrounding donations by companies to the Conservative Party and the regulation of donations by trade unions to the Labour Party could hardly be more marked. As the Minority Report points out, the Companies Act of 1985 requires companies to disclose in their Directors' Report political donations exceeding £200, although they can have leeway of up to two years after the event before the report need be lodged at Companies House. A shareholder has a right to question such donations at an AGM, but a resolution on the subject cannot be tabled without the support of 5 per cent of the voting rights or one hundred shareholders with paid-up capital of £100 or more. There is no provision in company law for a political fund, although in many cases the major shareholders are pension funds which presumably include people of all political colours, in whose interests their funds are supposedly managed. Decisions on political donations may be taken by directors without any reference being made to shareholders, and there is no provision whatsover for shareholders who dissent from such a donation being made to opt out.

Theoretically, says the Minority Report, dissident shareholders can sue for breach of duty, but in relation to political donations this, so far as they could ascertain, has never been tested in law. In addition the Companies Act makes no provision for unincorporated associations to declare political donations.

In contrast, all trade union members must now be allowed to opt out of the political levy, if they so wish, and all contributions to political parties or organisations must appear in the up-to-date audited and published accounts of a union.

Over the years Labour Research has continued its search for company donors and in its January 1994 issue reveals a further £1.6m going to the Conservatives from 102 companies during the preceding two years. This included two special election-year donations of £100,000 from the Yorkshire property developer Stadium City and the bakery and food group George Weston. Altogether in recent years Labour Research tracked down £4.9m in election donations from 311 companies. The companies cover a very wide range, from Allied Lyons, the Argyll Group, Black and Decker and Boddingtons through Hambros Bank to Kelloggs, Weetabix and Whitbread.

In 1992 the newly privatised Thames Water donated £50,000 to party funds, which led to a large number of complaints from consumers. Thames Customer Service Committee took the view that 'political donations (like very high salaries to senior company staff and Chairman) left a nasty taste in the mouth and were unpopular, very unpopular, with water customers'.

In the run up to the 1992 election the party also received a donation from Michael Green, head of Carlton Television and subsequently a successful bidder for one of the TV franchises. (Carlton has since taken over Thames TV as well and has a 36 per cent stake in ITN.)[8]

Apparently Labour Research 'also traced that very rare phenomenon – two company donations to the Labour Party'. Since 1990, stores and pools group Littlewoods has been a substantial supporter of the Conservative Party, while also giving small sums to the Liberal Democrats. However, in election year, it cut down on its overall contributions, gave £7,450 to the Conservatives, £2,400 to the Liberal Democrats and just £1,200 to the Labour Party. The other Labour Party donation, of £1,000, came from motor car dealer Curfin Investments.

Honours

'It has been suggested that there is a relationship between political donations and honours,' says the Minority Report. 'There is nothing new in this suggestion . . . governments of every political persuasion have tended to honour those who put money in the coffers of the ruling party.' Indeed there was a tremendous outcry at the time over Harold Wilson's last Honours Lists, in which a number of the mediocre and/or doubtful received knighthoods and peerages – the sobriquet 'Lord Gannex' comes immediately to mind.

According to evidence presented to the Home Affairs Committee Report between the election of Mrs Thatcher in 1979 and the 1993 New Year's Honours List, eighteen life peerages and eighty-two knighthoods have been given to industrialists connected with seventy-six companies which, over the same period, jointly donated £17.4m to the party or its front companies.

The largest donor, United Biscuits (£1,004,500) boasted one peerage and one knighthood, Hansons (£852,000) two peerages, Taylor Woodrow (£837,362) one peerage, one knighthood, British and Commonwealth (£823,56) one peerage, P & O (£727,500) one peerage, three knighthoods, Glaxo (£600,000) two knighthoods and Trafalgar House (£590,000) two peerages and one knighthood. Of the two major company donators who did not appear in the Honours List, George Weston Holdings (£820,000) and Western United Investments (£620,900), one is headed by a Canadian and the other has at its helm a hereditary peer, Lord Vestey.

Questioned as to whether or not there was a connection between the granting of honours and donations to the party, Sir Norman Fowler was adamant that all honours for political services were scrutinised by an independent committee of Privy Councillors. 'All political honours must be certificated to the effect that no payment or expectation of payment to any party or political fund is directly or indirectly associated with that recommendation.' Yet Lord Carr of Hadley, a member of that very committee, asked on a BBC radio programme if it was merely coincidence that businessmen who donated funds were honoured, replied, 'Yes, er, and yet it can't be as simple as that, can it?' Lord Shackleton, a former member of the same committee, told the *Observer* (27.6.93) that secret donations might well escape such scrutiny. 'There is an obvious gap here. It is likely that these secret donations are bypassing the scrutiny system and that honours are, effectively, being bought.'

The Minority Report notes that gossip about honours-for-sale dates back to the days of Lloyd George. It goes back way beyond that, even to before William the Conqueror rewarded his invading Norman knights. Perhaps, though, we might consider returning to the overt system introduced on the accession of James I in 1603. The king, looking around for means to fund his lavish lifestyle and finding the coffers somewhat bare, instituted a new deal. For an agreed sum you could buy the honour of your choice. The going price for a knighthood was set at £30 and James soon created some 838 new knights. For £1,095 you could buy the new rank of baronet and so on, up the scale. Within a comparatively short time the king had created three dukes, one marquess, thirty-two earls, nineteen viscounts and fifty-six barons, all strictly for cash down, and his Treasury soon benefited to the tune of £120,000.

At least it was common knowledge, though public discussion was not encouraged. In 1605 a play by Ben Jonson and George Chapman, *Eastward Hoe!*, so offended the king by, among other things, its derogatory references to the 'King's thirty-pound knights', that the two luckless dramatists were sent to prison. On his release at the beginning of November of that year, Jonson immediately attended a party thrown by an earlier group with a desire to clean up Parliament, the conspirators in the forthcoming Gunpowder Plot. But that's another story.

Chapter 4

TRUSTING IN THE NHS

The major reorganisation of the National Health Service was vitally necessary, we were told, in order to cut out waste and bureaucracy, and to put its services on a sensible market footing. To this end businessmen were encouraged to sit on its many Quangos; Regional Health Authorities ceased to consist of those elected to them from various sections of the community, becoming Quangos made up of government appointees; and the public no longer had access to their meetings and deliberations. Accountability, like so much else, was considered unnecessary. 'Value for money' was the buzz phrase, while we drowned in a flood of statistics showing how wonderful everything was, even if this was belied by personal experience.

Unhappily there are now all too many major and scandalous examples of what has happened in the NHS when accountability goes out of the window and greed and secrecy come in at the door, the whole coupled with gross mismanagement. As well as a host of tacky scandals, millions of pounds of taxpayers' money, so urgently required for patients, have been proved to have been wasted. It would be possible to write an entire book using nothing but examples of what has occurred in the National Health Service, but since this is not the object of this particular exercise, it is proposed to look at one in detail and mention others briefly.

The example in the frame is that of one of the country's largest Regional Health Authorities (RHAs), its Chairman who was proud of his reputation for cutting NHS services and who refused to resign as scandal mounted on scandal, the wasting of enormous sums of money, backdoor deals, four major investigations into what was going on and, finally, a Secretary of State for Health who, at the end of the whole débâcle, warmly congratulated the Chairman on his devotion to the NHS.

Ackers' Axe

Sir James Ackers was knighted in 1987 for 'services to the National Health Service'. A businessman whose firm, Ackers Jarrett, had become highly profitable from leasing out trucks and refuse vehicles to local authorities, he was a prominent Midlands Conservative. In the early 1980s he was invited to join the NHS National Policy Board and in 1982 was appointed Chairman of the West Midlands Regional Health Authority. His knighthood was followed, in 1990, by his reappointment as Chairman of the West Midlands RHA for an unprecedented third term. The chair of the RHA, a nice little earner bringing in £20,000 a year for a two-day week, was not Sir James' only Quango. He also sat on the Monopolies and Mergers Commission, the National Economic Development Council and was President of the National Association of Chambers of Commerce.

In a profile in the *Birmingham Post* (17.8.91), Sir James spoke of his warm friendship with Kenneth Clarke, who, as Secretary of State for Health, was responsible for implementing the massive changes in the NHS. Apparently he shares Mr Clarke's liking for tobacco and good living, and the accompanying picture shows him at his desk puffing away at a cigarette. 'Sir James has always kept a well-stocked drinks cupboard in his RHA office,' writes the *Post*'s medical correspondent, Jon Hunt. We are indebted to Jon Hunt and an investigation team from the *Birmingham Post*, as without their tenacity over the best part of three years it is unlikely much of what went on at the RHA would ever have come out; they were also in large part responsible for the series of investigations which later took place. At a time when investigative journalism of the proper sort is endlessly disparaged, it is a credit to the *Post* editor and his team.

Sir James was an energetic RHA Chairman, taking 'a notoriously firm hand with District Health Authorities, ordering them to balance their books even if it meant bed closures' (*Birmingham Post* 17.8.91). Between 1989 and 1990 senior officer after senior officer left in a major shake-up within the RHA. Ackers embraced the new NHS reforms whole-heartedly and soon the phrase 'Ackers' axe' became common currency in the region as services were slashed. He liked to be known as a man with 'an iron grip on affairs'. Ordinary people or RHA employees who tried to put their case to him or even requested consultation were met with what they describe as a wall of impenetrable jargon. By the time Ackers had been appointed Chairman for a third term he had a dream scheme in mind – the closure of all Birmingham's hospitals, their facilities to be transferred to one megasite, next to the existing Queen Elizabeth Hospital on the edge of Birmingham University campus. His position seemed absolutely secure. Yet by the beginning of 1993, when he was finally put under pressure to resign, he had presided over one of the biggest series of financial scandals ever to hit the NHS.

The trail of woe began in March 1990 when Sir James, accompanied by his colourful Director of Regionally Managed Services, Chris Watney, had dinner at the Post House Hotel, Great Barr, Birmingham, with a team of American consultants, the United Research Group. The dinner had been set up by Mr Watney, who had URG in mind to undertake a major efficiency study into the West Midlands RHA. The dinner was a great success and the very next day Chris Watney and the RHA's Senior Director of Finance, Martin Davies, signed a deal with a representative of URG for them to undertake the study for a fee of £2.5m. This was justified both then and subsequently on the grounds that the American experts would save the RHA at least £50m. When news of the arrangement leaked out, not everyone in the RHA felt so happy: an insider was later to tell the Audit Commission, after commenting that the sheer level of financial mismanagement was breathtaking, 'They were offered prices of between £20,000 and £100,000 for a contract, but they chose one which cost over £2m and it's not even clear what it was supposed to achieve.' This person went on to say that it seemed inexplicable in terms of mismanagement and suggestd the police should look into it. In a memo acquired by the *Post* written the day after the Post House dinner, Mr Watney described it as having been 'a very useful session' between himself, Sir James and URG.

Throughout the summer of 1990 'Ackers' axe' attracted no little attention as protests mounted over closures and senior staff were made redundant. Two such were Mrs Ann Coulson and Mr David Hands. As Sir James put it, 'We came to the conclusion that in the new RHA structure there was no call for either of these two posts.' Mrs Coulson, who was to have been responsible for overseeing the way District Health Authorities handled their money, was a Labour Councillor in Birmingham in the 1970s and the party's local Social Services spokeswoman.

On 31 July 1990 the new-look RHA announced it was to cut drastically the number of meetings held in public. This provoked anger which Sir James countered by saying that the new authority would be aiming to meet two-monthly and that members would be able to discuss matters in between. 'I don't think this will mean more closed access. I don't think anyone could complain about lack of access.' The RHA had previously had sixteen lay members. Now it had only five, along with four RHA officers and Sir James. So open was the access that the Chair of the consumers' watchdog, West Birmingham Community Health Council, was not even informed of its first meeting. 'Nothing was sent to me.' Commenting on the arrangements for the new RHA, Matthew Taylor, Director of the West Midlands Health Services Monitoring Unit, said of the old one, 'It is difficult to shed tears for an authority that had, in any case, become a rubber stamp for Sir James Ackers.'

In October 1990 it was rumoured that the Managing Director of the RHA, Ken Bales, would soon be seeking early retirement and that he was being pressured into resignation by both the Department of Health and the RHA, as it was considered he was insufficiently enthusiastic about the NHS reforms; what was wanted was someone who would take a lead. In the event he hung on for several months, in spite of the fact that, according to an unnamed RHA spokesperson, 'He has not been the flavour of the month for many years.'

In January 1991 came the first hint that all was not well with the West Midlands RHA. A faulty computer began sending out unauthorised cheques totalling almost £1m. For some firms it was a veritable bonanza as they received duplicate payments. The first prize would undoubtedly have gone to Boss Warehouse, whose invoice for £143,842 was processed four times, except that one official realised what had happened and stopped the cheque being sent out. In other cases, money had to be retrieved, including £386,120 from Digital DEC and £42,500 from Liverpool & Victoria Assurance, both payments having been processed twice. Department of Health auditors later called in to help clean up the mess said that they were unable to form an opinion on the accuracy of the RHA's accounts for the year 1989–90 owing to there being 'so many mistakes'.

According to the Audit Commission, brought in later, 'Absence of certain controls caused payments to be made without proper authorisation and without proper supporting documentation.' Questioned at the time about the computer mistakes by the *Coventry Evening Telegraph*, Director of Finance Martin Davies replied, 'An exercise to retrospectively check all payments in 1989–90 is nearing completion. The results to date are very encouraging and there is no evidence to substantiate any significant duplication. All items of doubt are being followed up and there are no losses to report to the Authority.' His confidence would later prove to have been misplaced.

In April 1991, in an effort to bring the £500m hospital megascheme nearer, the RHA merged its two largest District Health Authorities, Central Birmingham and South Birmingham.

By the summer of 1991 West Midlands RHA was faced with a torrent of complaints from District Health Authorities over the way the RHA had used the new internal market system (through which they were supposed to purchase its services) to raise its prices drastically. So persistent was the clamour that eventually Sir James found himself having to set up what would be the first of a series of inquiries into the workings of the RHA. First off was the Carver Inquiry, a committee headed by Roy Carver, Chairman of Wolverhampton Health Authority.

It was during the inquiries by the Carver Committee that light was shone on the URG consultancy. So far from vast savings of £50m, it was beginning to look as though the cost to the taxpayer for the search for such a saving was rapidly reaching £4m. Within no time URG had run up an expenses bill of £350,000, which included the leasing of expensive houses in London for executives and their wives, hotel bills at the most pricey hotels for executives visiting Birmingham, private aircraft to fly them to work, and bills for lavish meals washed down with expensive wine. Carver's committee later uncovered another project hitherto unknown to the public, Healthtrac. The contract, apparently signed in August 1991 at a cost of nearly £4m, was designed as 'an electronic trading system' to link all hospital wards with a massive central supply depot at King's Norton on the outskirts of Birmingham. Faced by what he considered to be an alarming situation, Carver recommended an investigation by the District Auditor on behalf of the Audit Commisison. Thus, as the furore over closures continued to grow as Sir James wielded his axe on a ward here and a bed there, he was now facing two investigations into the possibility that the RHA had mishandled millions of pounds of public money.

Sir James had been pressured into setting up the Carver Inquiry following a secret internal one which had reported in June. It was at this point that Chris Watney decided to seek early retirement.

In July 1991 the first rumours began to circulate that Sir James himself was about to resign.[1] These rumours were to provide the leitmotiv of media reports over the next two years. Neither Dame Nellie Melba nor Frank Sinatra was ever rumoured so frequently to be on the point of retirement. Certainly during that month senior RHA officers met in an emergency session to discuss the growing crisis, although no decision was reached. Sir James, meanwhile, was keeping what was described as 'a low profile' at a house in Tamworth, his flat in Sutton Coldfield having suddenly been emptied of furniture in the course of a single night. Tracked down by sleuths from the *Post* on the night of 21 July, Sir James' wife came to the door saying, 'This is private property. Please leave. He is not in.' The following Friday he cancelled a promised visit to a Wolverhampton hospital. An anonymous RHA source told the media that Sir James was very upset because of 'high-level' pressure on him to resign. 'It is very unusual indeed for managers to meet in such a way to consider the position of their chairman' commented the source.

But Sir James did not resign. 1991 was, however, to prove, in the words used by the Queen, an *annus horribilis* for him. In August came the annoucement: 'Health Chief Ackers calls in Receivers'.[2] On 16 August two receivers from accountants Arthur Andersen's of Birmingham took control of Ackers Jarrett to investigate the extent of the company's debts. Sir James had 24,000 shares in his company, the largest shareholder being a Mr John Edwards, who, only a month earlier, had denied the company had any problems. The Company Secretary, Sir Patrick Lawrence, had only recently chaired a national Conservative Party Conference. He and Sir James were described as 'major power brokers in the region's business and social establishment'.

It was suggested that one of the reasons the company, which had had a turnover of £23m a year, had run into difficulties was that the previous May it had paid £6.25m for its rival, Truckrent of Leicester, thus overstretching the company during the recession when interest rates were high. Following suggestions that since Sir James was responsible for one of the biggest health budgets in the country, £1.4bn, perhaps it was time he stood down, he again made it clear that where the RHA was concerned he was 'staying put': 'The Ackers Jarrett position is entirely separate from my responsibilities to the Regional Health Authority. I have discussed this with Ministers and with colleagues and I confirm that I will be continuing as chairman.'[3]

A week after the collapse of the company Sir James was again refusing to resign, this time when local MPs presented him with a 100,000-signature petition protesting at the plans for the opting out of the East Birmingham Hospital.

In September 1991 Qa Business Services, the RHA's privatised computer division, collapsed and was taken over by AT&T Istel who, by this time, had also been called in to work on Healthtrac.

In the spring of 1992 the sky finally fell in on the West Midlands RHA. As well as investigations by the Carver Committee and the District Auditor, there was shortly to be a third inquiry. By April 1992 the new combined District Health Authority of South and

Central Birmingham, set up to see through the £500m hospital megaproject, was found to have run up an overdraft of £30m. Another external auditor, KPMG Peat Marwick, was called in to examine what had gone wrong. It was to condemn the RHA's handling of the creation of the new authority as the prime cause of its financial problems.

At the end of August 1991 the District Auditor, Mr Keith Stanton, presented his first report to the RHA, instructing that it should publish at least one section of it. Four days beforehand the RHA's Finance Director and Deputy Managing Director, Martin Davies, resigned. He was, he said, planning to work as an independent financial consultant and his departure had nothing to do with the imminent publication of the District Auditor's report.

Much of what did come to light initially concerned Mr Chris Watney. He was not, however, on hand to answer the charges made against him.

'Come in, Mr Watney, it's time to explain yourself' was the *Post*'s headline over a cartoon of a yacht with the word 'Bounty' painted on her stern.[4] This was a reference to the fact that the ex-Director of Regionally Managed Services was currently enjoying a world cruise with his wife in his yacht. They had set sail a few weeks after he left the RHA and had last been heard of in Tahiti.

The District Auditor dealt first with the £2.5m URG contract and the lavish expenses paid out to its employees. The Auditor's report accused Mr Watney of 'a cavalier disregard for the standards of conduct expected from public officers'. It criticised the RHA for paying invoices without seeing most of the accounts, and continued, 'In 1986 the RHA set up a Members' Panel to keep an overview of its services. However, no terms of references were set, and the panel was ineffective. The director ignored the panel and did not report to the RHA board. The RHA chairman and members of the board said they did not know what was going on in respect of the supplies consultancy contract. No effective control was exercised over him [Mr Watney]. Despite the rule that all contracts over £50,000 must be under the seal of the RHA, this contract, for £2.5m, was just a letter from the consultants telling Mr Watney what they would do and charge. The RHA board never even saw the letter.' The RHA then paid out £2.5m without specifying the staff who would work on the job or what the RHA would get for the money.

In the unpublished part of the report, a copy of which was leaked to the *Birmingham Post*, the District Auditor made a series of allegations regarding Mr Watney, which the paper later published in full (26.12.92). These were that he had had links with a business consultant, Mr Philip Vignoles, who had been paid an introductory fee of £80,000 for setting up the URG contract. Mr Watney had also been involved in a company called Laureat Search, of which both he and Mr Vignoles were directors. Mr Watney had also undertaken part-time work for a Suffolk-based luxury yacht-building company, Whisstocks, of which the ubiquitous Mr Vignoles was Chairman. It appeared that Mr Watney had used Mr Vignoles' services extensively when head-hunting for top RHA jobs.

Sir James was immediately asked about the published criticisms of Mr Watney and what he had to say about the way the URG affair had been handled. Sir James, who had always boasted of his hands-on way of working, replied that he had known nothing of what had gone on. He had not even been advised that a firm agreement had been reached with URG after the dinner at the Post House Hotel, Great Barr, although what passed for a contract had been signed the following morning. Pressed further as to whether Watney had actually taken early retirement or been sacked, and whether rumours were correct that he had received a massive golden handshake, Sir James finally conceded that Mr Watney had been asked to leave and his post declared redundant; he declined to comment regarding the golden handshake. As to the notorious Post House dinner at which the 'contract' had been discussed, he had no idea who had paid for it, but it was only a 'modest, three-course affair'. And no, he would not be resigning. He saw no reason to do so.

Regarding Mr Watney, it was also noted that the 'soft-spoken church treasurer' had not declared a troubled episode from his past when he applied for his job with the RHA.[5] He told them in his job applications that he had spent the years 1980–83 working as a management consultant. In fact in 1980 he was Managing Director of a Birmingham silverware firm, Cavalier Tableware. In 1981 the firm went into receivership and Mr Watney led a management buy-out which paid £850,000 for its assets. The following year the new company also went into receivership.

The District Auditor's report also claimed that Mr Watney had had a secret agenda to privatise parts of his department, one of which, Qa Business Services, involved with the ill-fated computer project, having gone into receivership the previous year. The Auditor was also due to report both on the controversial £3.5m Healthtrac computer programme and on the privatisation of the RHA's computer department, both of which were Mr Watney's responsibility. Martin Davies was heavily criticised for his lack of overall financial control. Again pressed on resignation, Sir James explained that this was unnecessary, as the trouble had arisen only because Mr Watney 'had misled colleagues and not told them what he was doing'. His own hands were clean. No, he would not resign.

Meanwhile Birmingham was facing a series of hospital closures as it was £12m in the red.

In October 1992 the Auditor General published a further report, which revealed why the *Post* cartoonist had labelled Watney's yacht the *Bounty*. On leaving the RHA after five years' service, Mr Watney had been given a substantial golden handshake, as well as an entitlement to a £6,647 annual pension. The golden handshake included an immediate lump sum of £19,387, and further payments totalling £62,005: a £20,147 redundancy payment, a payment in lieu of notice of £12,876 and a special payment of £28,982 to compensate for an earlier error in calculating his pension. The total amount came to £81,392, in addition to the pension. But the Auditor, following consultation with the Department of Health, ruled that the RHA had incorrectly calculated the redundancy payment, as NHS regulations made no provision for the special payment. Nor had the RHA given approval for the payment. It was, therefore, seeking legal advice on how to recover the 'irregular payment' of £41,500.

The Auditor then went on to criticise the RHA over the merger of the Central and South Birmingham Health Authorities, which had created a new authority, now £10.5m in the red. 'The region should have ensured that the financial situations of the authorities were fully taken into account in the merger.' It was also revealed that when Martin Davies had resigned in September, he had received six months' pay in lieu of notice and two months' pay in lieu of untaken leave, a sum in the region of £20,000. On the same date that part of the Auditor's report was published, patients and staff from Birmingham hospitals were travelling to London to lobby MPs and present the government with a petition against the closure of Birmingham's famous Accident and Royal Orthopaedic Hospitals.

A leader in the *Coventry Evening Telegraph* said that the conduct of senior officers of the RHA 'defied belief. With regard to the URG consultants – lavish entertaining, top hotels, expensive wine – the consultants spared no cost. They did not, however, come up with the goods . . . That the RHA, a body charged with allocating taxpayers' scarce resources for patient care should behave in such a way is outrageous. The public has a right to hear explanations from the RHA's two top directors who have resigned over the affair . . . the inquiry should also examine the role of RHA Chairman, Sir James Ackers, who has so far disclaimed responsibility for the débâcle.'

Within days the Department of Health announced that it would be sending its own investigators, led by Sir Roy Griffiths, one of the government's chief architects of Health Service reforms. Sir Roy would work with the RHA 'to help it discharge its role efficiently and effectively'. Asked if this might now mean his resignation, Sir James replied that since neither he nor his board had authorised the URG contract, he had no intention of resigning.

Meanwhile attempts to reach the elusive Mr Watney were proving unsuccessful. On 27 October an RHA spokesman admitted, 'The last communication we had from him was to say that he was somewhere near the Cook Islands, heading for New Zealand.' Mr Watney's solicitors said that he was shortly planning to return to Britain to answer his critics.

Two days later, Sir James attended 'crisis talks' in London over the apparently endless stream of damning reports, slipping away from the meeting afterwards without making any comment. The talks had involved Sir Roy Griffiths, Health Minister Dr Brian Mawhinney, who had consistently refused to intervene in the affair and, for a short time, Secretary of State Virginia Bottomley herself. Asked later about Sir James's future, Mrs Bottomley replied, 'Sir James joined me in welcoming Sir Roy's assistance. The NHS management executive is working closely with the RHA to ensure all the lessons are identified and applied.'

By then the scandal had reached Parliament and Shadow Health spokesman David Blunkett had written to Mrs Bottomley demanding Sir James' resignation, while eighteen Labour MPs had signed an Early Day Motion calling on him to go. As Labour MP Robin Corbett put it, 'We are no longer able to afford Sir James and he should quit.' One Conservative MP, Michael Fabricant, felt that the money that was wasted should have gone on nurses and hospitals. But Mr James Pewsey, Conservative MP for Rugby and Kenilworth said, 'The Audit Commission report contains no criticism of Sir James, indeed it says he took the appropriate action at the time. Non-executive directors have backed him ... this is a very substantial vote of confidence.' It seems Mrs Bottomley agreed, for she refused to be drawn on his future.[6]

As Parliament discussed the West Midlands RHA, 130 employees of its failed privatised computer department, Qa Business Services, learned they would receive only a third of their pension entitlements, after trustees revealed a £2.2m deficit in the fund. Solicitors acting for the pension fund trustees said, 'This is not a Maxwell situation, there is no suggestion of fraud.'

Finally, at the end of November, Mr Watney returned and immediately set about demolishing Sir James' statements that he had been unaware of the signing, terms and conditions of the URG contract. 'I did not make any decisions on my own,' he said, 'it would have been totally incorrect to do so. Our division had its own board with RHA members on it. The URG consultancy was discussed with the Chairman, the Regional Managing Director, the Director of Finance and the Director of Personnel.' He claimed there was an official NHS contract and he intended to find it. Minutes of different RHA boards would support his case. He personally thought that expenses of the order of 10 per cent of the cost of the entire contract were 'about right'.

Questioned about the role played by Mr Vignoles in setting up the contract, Mr Watney claimed to have no knowledge of this, for 'if you work in the public sector you have to be whiter than white'. Asked about his other involvements with Mr Vignoles he said that when he agreed to take on the RHA job it had been on the 'clear understanding I was able to carry out certain other outside interests . . . I was encouraged in this by the Chairman because it helped me keep my hand in at business.' He agreed he had initiated the £3.5m Healthtrac contract, but it had been implemented after he had left. As to the supposed overpayment to him of over £40,000, no, he had no intention whatsoever of paying it back.[7]

It was then decided that the House of Commons Public Accounts Committee should look into the matter of West Midlands RHA. This would run parallel to the other inquiries and those now being undertaken by the police. It was likely that both Ackers and Watney would be called.

1993 dawned with Sir James still in post while the series of damning reports from Carver, Peat Marwick, the District Auditor and through him the Audit Commission, Sir Roy Griffiths and the Department of Health continued to pile up.

In November 1992 the *Post* had revealed yet further areas of disquiet. First, that a senior official from the RHA's supplies department was married to a sales representative from Healthtrac, the company which had won the £3.5m contact and which was now virtually defunct, and that a £300,000 loan had been made earlier in the year by the RHA to an organisation called Financial Information Packages, which had been floated as an independent company from a small division of the RHA. The firm, run by a charity, the Health Management Trust, was started with a £630,000 loan from the RHA and £440,000 in subscriptions from District Health Authorities. By 1991 it had been £300,000 in the red, whereupon the RHA had stepped in with yet another loan. By early January 1993 the Audit Commission was investigating whether this had been a lawful use of public money. Sources within the RHA revealed that frantic meetings were now being held at the RHA between Sir James and his directors.

Finally, on 8 January 1993, Sir James fell on his own axe.

His long-drawn-out resignation prompted a fulsome letter from Virginia Bottomley, dated 8.1.93. 'Dear Jim,' she wrote, 'Thank you for your letter asking to relinquish your office of Chairman of

West Midlands RHA. It is characteristically good of you to offer to make way for some new blood to take forward the work you have begun.' He had, she said, served the NHS with commitment, led many improvements in the West Midlands where 'waiting lists have dramatically fallen' and strongly supported the NHS reforms. 'In addition you have recently initiated some important improvements in the managerial structure of this region. Underpinning all this has been your personal commitment to the Health Service and its patients ... Let me express my appreciation and that of my predecessors for all that you have done for the Health Service over many years and I wish you well for the future. Yours ever, Virginia.'

Not a mention from the lady who always has statistics at her fingertips on the need to save every penny for 'patient care' of the millions of pounds of wasted taxpayers' money. Shortly afterwards it was revealed that Sir James would receive a golden handshake of somewhere between £20,000–£30,000.

A reporter from the *Health Services Journal* watched the last act – as at the time of writing – in the saga of West Midlands RHA as the Commons' Public Accounts Committee deliberated the matter. Sir James blamed administrative confusion, the sheer size of the region, and failure by others to carry out instructions. The then NHS Chief Executive, Sir Duncan Nichol, admitted that the whole thing had been a shambles and, asked by MP Alan Williams if he thought Sir James should have been sacked, replied, 'It's not for me to comment.' Mr Terry Davis MP pointed out that of the senior executives involved in the URG débâcle, Mr Bales had been allowed to retire early, Martin Davies had left with a lump sum of £43,000, Mr Mel Nock, who had authorised the overpayment to Mr Watney, had merely been given a formal warning and Mr Watney had sailed off round the world. 'That doesn't seem right to me, does it to you?' he asked Sir Duncan.

'I'm not going to comment on that,' Sir Duncan replied, 'you have to take all the facts into account.'

Did he realise it was felt that there had been a cover-up?

'No, I don't,' insisted Sir Duncan.

Mr Davies went on to enquire why three separate versions of the Auditor's Report had been published: one for the Public Accounts

Committee, one for the RHA and one for the public. Sir Duncan did not know why, nor why Mr Watney had been receiving performance-related pay even though he repeatedly overspent his budget.

Commenting on the recent history of the West Midlands Regional Health Authority as a whole, the HSSJ described what had happened as 'an incompetent shambles which smelt of a gravy train. It was incredible, astonishing, curious, strange and rotten.'

As the Public Accounts Committee commented in its report, *The Proper Conduct of Public Business*, published in January 1994, serious shortcomings in management, control and accountability had led to the waste of millions of pounds 'at the expense of health care for sick people in the West Midlands. The essence of this mismanagement was that the responsible official . . . was able to follow his own path, making a bonfire of the rules in the process, uncontrolled either by the RHA or senior management.' It went on to accuse Sir James and members of his RHA of 'seriously neglecting their duty'.

Wessex RHA and Other Examples

While the saga of West Midlands RHA is among the more spectacular débâcles of the new NHS, it was not the most expensive. That prize is awarded to Wessex RHA for incurring losses of £63m on failed attempts to integrate all information technology systems in its region. The story of what went wrong would match the West Midlands tale in length but, briefly, after investigations by the Audit Commission and the Public Accounts Committee, what happened was described as 'a litany of bungling, incompetence and possible deceit'. Special criticism was reserved for the RHA's unaccountability and the fact that the company which was advising the RHA on which computer system to buy was also bidding for the contract and may well have had inside information. The contract was then awarded to the company at an inquorate meeting of the RHA, a contract which contained no quality provisions and no maximum price. Wessex Integrated Systems, which had won the contract to operate the system, had a contract guaranteeing 15 per cent profits, regardless of performance and without any controls. Also, if the company failed, the RHA undertook to step in. The Public Accounts Committee noted that 'fundamental changes are needed in the management and accountability arrangements at RHAs.'[8]

A former Regional Estates Director at South West Thames RHA, with a salary of around £40,000, was able to use knowledge acquired there to make a personal profit of £900,000 when his hived-off department was sold to a consultancy group. Tony Bristow, who was also Chairman and Managing Director of Estates Design and Management Ltd, had a 55 per cent stake in the company, which was sold to the Capital Group plc in 1992 for £1.7m in cash and shares. The RHA vigorously defended its action in privatising the department after a catalogue of criticism from the District Auditor. The RHA denied acting 'irresponsibly', but agreed that the £1.7m profit from the sale was a 'foregoing of potential benefit'. It also admitted ignoring advice from KPMG Peat Marwick who recommended competitive tendering.[9]

More than £100,000 of NHS money was unlawfully spent assisting a health manager's move to a new appointment, the District Auditor discovered after being called in to investigate a 'relocation package' offered by Cheshire RHA. The former Halton Authority spent a total of £228,129 of taxpayers' money underwriting the moving costs of its General Manager, Tony Anstey, from October 1989 to the autumn of 1993. The Auditor commented, 'The question needs to be posed as to whether this level of support was in the best interests of the inhabitants of Halton.' The money represented interest on bridging loans, removal expenses and another, unspecified, interest-free loan. The news came on the same day that the trial of businessmen accused of defrauding Wessex RHA of £40,000 had been abandoned after ten weeks, due to conflict of evidence. The trial, which will have to be reordered, has already cost £2m.[10]

In May 1994 the National Audit Office revealed that a Health Authority had covered up a £70,000 payment to a manager who had left the service after presiding over huge losses. Mike Shannon, former General Manager of Warrington District Hospital, received his pay-off under a deal which included a confidentiality clause. The Audit Office's investigation followed a parliamentary question from Labour MP Mike Hall which Health Ministers had refused to answer: it included a query on why Mr Shannon had been promoted on the day he was declared redundant! Looked into further by the Public Accounts Committee, it was revealed that a 'gagging clause' had gone with the overpayment, although the Health Authority had taken a serious view of Mr Shannon's failure to manage the financial position of the acute unit. Under the deal he received £32,314, the use of a government-owned car from 1 July 1992 to 31 March 1993, and a payment of £6,594 for being sacked; he was then given a lump sum of £24,546 superannuation and an £8,182 pension, and asked to sign the gagging clause.[11]

In November 1992 the Prime Minister was asked to sack Welsh Health Minister Gwilym Jones for making 'political appointments'. Labour MP Rhodri Morgan pointed out that the Minister had selected his secretary, Carolyn Jones, as a member of South Glamorgan Health Authority at a salary of £5,000 for two days' work a week. Mrs Jones was married to the Minister's election agent, David Jones. Mr Gwilym Jones also appointed Janet Sainsbury, wife of the leader of the Tory group on Cardiff Council, to the Chair of South Glamorgan Family Services Authority. Mr Morgan pointed out that both Mr Sainsbury and Mr Jones were members of the Wenallt Masonic Lodge of which Mr Gwilym Jones was 'chief steward'. A spokesman for the Welsh Office, commenting on the Masonic connection, said, 'A fair-minded person might say it was just coincidence.'[12]

On 23 September 1993 it was announced that Sir Duncan Nichol was to join the board of the private health group BUPA. Sir Duncan had, until six months previously, been the Chief Executive of the National Health Service. His tenure of office had become increasingly controversial as in his capacity as a senior civil servant he gave whole-hearted and vocal support to the government's

Health Service reforms. It has obviously caused disquiet that the man who was until recently running the NHS has now moved over to an organisation devoted entirely to private care. Nor is this all. Sir Duncan is also Chairman of a Quango, Healthcare 2000, a commission of inquiry into the future of health provision, which is funded by drugs companies. BUPA will not say how much Sir Duncan will be paid. Speaking on the BBC *Today* programme on the day of the announcement, Sir Duncan denied that any conflict of interest could be involved. Under present rules, high-ranking civil servants must obtain government approval for any such employment taken up within two years of leaving their posts. Outside appointments should be subject to scrutiny, particularly when the prospective employer has had any kind of financial or contractual arrangement with the civil servant's former department or where the person 'could be or could be thought to be significantly helpful to the employer in dealing with matters where policy is developing'.

Junior Health Minister Tom Sackville, quoted in the *Guardian* on the day Sir Duncan's appointment was announced, said, 'This appointment is a matter for BUPA and Sir Duncan. There is positive benefit to the NHS in close co-operation with the private sector and I am sure Sir Duncan will be valuable there.'

The radical changes to the NHS were sold on the basis that market forces, i.e. the internal market, would make it leaner and fitter and do away with unnecessary bureaucracy, although, in fact, the administrative costs of the old NHS were among the lowest for any health service in the world. Likewise, it was also decided that selected experts from the world of business were better fitted to make decisions on the way it was run than the former system whereby a substantial number of elected members sat on the relevant committees. As these few examples have shown, not only do we now have a top-heavy bureaucracy, but the opportunities for mismanagement and wasteful expenditure by unelected bodies have substantially increased, along with opportunities for the misuse of public funds.

Chapter 5

VOTE EARLY, VOTE OFTEN

In the eighteenth century the Pitt family bought the ancient Cornish estate of Boconnoc on the upper reaches of the Fowey River. They had been able to purchase it at a bargain price from a Lady Mohun whose extravagant and dissolute husband, addicted to gambling, had been killed in a duel following accusations of cheating at cards. The Pitts had two reasons for acquiring the estate: one was in order to become large country landowners; the other that both sons, Thomas and William, were eager to get into politics. They had privately surveyed all the country's rotten boroughs and had discovered that the most corrupt area of the lot was Cornwall. In 1754, with a population of only 135,000, Cornwall returned no fewer than forty-four MPs. Tiny Fowey, on the edge of the Boconnoc estate, returned two, voted in by just forty-odd men who were eligible to vote. As a rule these two seats circulated among the area's large landowners, the Trefrys, the Rashleighs and the Edgecumbes.

When, in 1746, Thomas Pitt attempted to 'buy' one of the two Fowey seats, spending over £2,000 trying to persuade the forty-five worthies to vote for him, the Cornish landowners closed ranks. The Fowey voters happily took Thomas's money and allowed him to wine and dine them, but returned their own local gentry. Wining and dining was commonplace and an account still exists for the crates of port and brandy purchased by a Helston parliamentary candidate. Others took different measures. Forty or so miles from Fowey, in the far west port of Hayle, the sitting MP did not bother with bribes. As he owned most of the property in the town he simply told his tenants that if they did not vote for him, they would promptly be evicted. They took the hint.

It is ironic, therefore, that it was Hayle, in the St Ives constituency, that featured so prominently in the events following the April 1992 general election and the district elections of 7 May. In spite of a police investigation lasting months, the situation has never been satisfactorily resolved, leaving continuing disquiet in the area, coupled with national concern that, unless precautions are taken before the next general election, there is nothing to stop the same thing happening again.

What happened centres around proxy votes and has implications well outside the boundaries of the constitutency of St Ives. Proxy votes were designed to aid those who are elderly or disabled, and thus unable easily to get to a polling station, to designate a proxy, usually a relative or close friend, to vote on their behalf. Under electoral law, anyone who canvasses for votes on the doorstep and collects forms for proxy voters must make it clear then and there what they are doing and which party they represent. This is essential, for signing a proxy form does not mean that the person wants a proxy vote just for that particular election. It means that they have, in effect, handed over their vote in perpetuity. (In this, a proxy vote differs from a postal vote, which has to be applied for each time.) It is all perfectly legal and above board, but it does assume that everyone involved acts in good faith and it is obvious that the system could be open to abuse.

In any election, general or local, there are some mistakes and it should be said at once that there were two minor cases of breaches in the law at St Ives in 1992. A Liberal Democrat worker applied for three proxy votes on behalf of Liberal Democrat voters, discovered that only two might be applied for by any proxy and duly reported her error to the Returning Officer. A Labour worker applied for a proxy instead of a postal vote for a known Labour voter and, again, had to admit an error.

The proxy votes which are the subject of this chapter, however, were all applied for by the local Conservative Association and were on an altogether different scale. In total some 133 proxy votes are in dispute and fifty of those alleged to have applied for them say they have never heard of the people voting on their behalf;

seventeen postal vote forms were clumsily altered with Tippex so that they became proxy vote applications, the proxies in question being prominent Conservative Party activists; and, strangest of all, five dead people apparently managed to communicate across the Great Divide to persuade local Tories to vote on their behalf.

At one point on general election day, two St Ives polling stations were registering complaints at the rate of twenty an hour, while within a week police at Camborne headquarters found themselves inundated with requests that they should investigate possible electoral fraud.

As regards the April 1992 general election, a hundred or so dodgy votes would not have altered the result. That said, however, the political situation has changed dramatically in the St Ives constituency in recent times. Thirty years ago it returned an MP who described himself on the charge sheet as a 'National Liberal Conservative', thus presumably hoping to scoop up the votes of Nationalists, Liberals and Conservatives, even though he operated out of the local Conservative office. When he retired, the Conservative candidate described himself simply as 'Conservative' – though it scarcely seemed to matter as in those days it was hardly necessary to organise a count, merely to weigh the Tory vote. Not any more: at the 1992 general election the Liberal Democrats slashed the large majority of the sitting Conservative MP, David Harris, down to a mere 1,600 votes, making it one of the country's most marginal seats. There were, on that occasion, just 1,600 proxy votes registered, although again it must be stressed, only a relatively small proportion of those are in dispute.

Sixteen hundred is quite a high number for proxy votes, particularly in an area with a low population, but St Ives is a constituency popular with retired people and with a large number of residential old people's homes. Indeed, when the first great wave of privatisation of council-run residential homes took place, many hoteliers and bed-and-breakfast landlords and landladies, hammered by the recession, changed from accommodating holidaymakers and converted their properties so that they might offer residential care. The Conservatives in the area have always taken a keen interest in the vote from residential homes and have worked hard to achieve as high a proportion as possible. Just how

St Ives compares with other areas in its number of proxies is hard to discover. Truro's Liberal Democrat MP, Matthew Taylor, asked the Home Office for the necessary statistics, but was told that these were not centrally collated.

However, while nobody is claiming that without the doubtful proxy votes the general election result would have been different, it was an altogether different matter where Penwith District Council, which includes the St Ives parliamentary constituency, was concerned. Steadily over the last ten years the Labour Party has made real inroads into the Conservative vote and before the 1992 elections had finally become the largest single party on the Council, running it in a loose coalition with other parties. The Conservatives were determined to wrench control back again. While there are odd instances of disputed votes elsewhere, nearly all those in contention were cast in the Hayle-Gwithian ward, which the Conservative candidate, Mrs Gillian Powell, won by nine votes. Her victory changed the balance of the Council, putting the Conservatives back in charge of all the crucial committees.[1] Mrs Powell really did need to win.

Within a few weeks of the 1992 election a number of other investigators as well as the police were looking into what was fast becoming the votes scandal. First on the scene, in spite of being handicapped by lack of resources, was Peter Wright-Davies, editor of Penwith's alternative monthly news magazine, *Voice*. He was soon joined by local and national newspaper journalists and teams from local and national TV, including BBC's *Spotlight South West*, based in Plymouth, and the networked programme *Newsnight*. The story that follows is based on their findings, plus taped and/or videoed interviews.

The main thrust of all the investigations centred around the Conservative victor of the Gwithian ward, Mrs Gillian Powell, who runs a taxi business. From the first interview within two or three days of the election results to the time of writing in the summer of 1994, Mrs Powell has remained consistent: that while she had specifically targeted old people's homes in her area, all those who gave her proxy votes had done so willingly and in the full knowledge that they were asking her to arrange for someone to vote Conservative for them; that she had applied no pressure on them; that all those who signed were fit to do so and in their right minds (though old people, as she pointed out, can be 'forgetful'); and that she knew nothing whatsoever of the Tippexed voting forms or the dead voters.

The local Conservative Party stated that it had always made a big effort to arrange proxy and postal votes and that if the other parties were now crying foul, then it was because they had not made the same efforts to garner in votes on their own account. Indeed, within days of the first burst of media publicity, the former Chairman of the St Ives Conservative Association, William Rogers, announced that the party had already held its own internal inquiry and found nothing amiss, but that if the current police investigation came up with anything which needed further investigation, the party would happily co-operate. He reiterated that the local Conservatives had always targeted old people's homes.

It seems that Mrs Powell had begun her campaign for proxy votes in the spring of 1991 and had been most assiduous in her efforts. Two residential homes had been paid particular attention, the Pinetrees on Connor Downs, just outside Hayle, and the Glencoe in St Ives. It was soon clear that the residents of Pinetrees were particularly up in arms. The home is only about a hundred yards from where the polling station was set up and some nine residents went down to vote on polling day. Seven were allowed to vote, two were not. Mrs Maud Henley was told she had already had a proxy vote and when she protested was told she could do nothing about it. She vaguely remembered signing some kind of a form flourished at her by Mrs Powell months earlier. 'I signed it in the end to get rid of her, I thought if I did so, she'd go away.' She was adamant that it had not been made clear to her that it was a proxy vote form or that she had assigned someone to vote Conservative for her. The name of the person voting on her behalf was a Mrs Eileen Hollabeck, of whom Mrs Henley had never heard. 'Let me get at her!' she told the film crew. No, she had never been asked if she would vote Conservative or, indeed, how she would vote. Nor, she stated firmly, would she have said if asked.

Mrs Betty Ellis was even more infuriated. When she was told she could not vote, 'I stood at the door . . . I couldn't believe it.

I've never missed voting in an election for fifty years.' Her daughter, Mrs Joyce Davenport, rang up the person supposedly nominated to vote for her mother, a Conservative activist called Ian Hayward. To her surprise she was called back by Mrs Powell who assured her that her mother had given her the right to assign her vote: 'She did agree . . . the trouble with old people is that they do forget.' But both Mrs Ellis and Mrs Davenport are adamant that Mrs Ellis would have done no such thing, for Mrs Ellis is the widow of a local Labour politician who had previously been Labour Mayor of Droylesden in Manchester. 'When I told them at the polling station that I had to vote, they said I'd already done so, by proxy. They took my voting card off me and tore it in half. They took away from me what I'd had all my life. I couldn't have a blinking vote. I think my husband would have turned in his blinking grave!'

All the seventeen forms on which it is clear that Tippex had been used to alter them from proxy to postal votes came from Pinetrees, a matter which greatly distressed the home's owners, Paul and Maureen Connolly. Both assured Mark Easton of *Newsnight* that they had always provided postal vote forms for residents who would find it difficult to vote in person, as postal votes seemed the fairest way of doing things. It did not give away for good the person's right to vote, it enabled them to change their mind if they wished and to feel in control of what they were doing. There was no question of any of the seventeen Pinetrees votes being proxies. Maureen Connolly said the names entered as proxies to vote for the residents were 'not there when we handed the forms in'. 'Are you sure?' Mark Easton pressed. 'Absolutely sure,' she replied. Her husband confirmed, 'The forms have definitely been altered.' They and the residents had assumed Mrs Powell would hand the forms in to the Council and had been surprised when it came to the general election and no postal votes had been received.

As Mrs Almeda Roach, a resident of Pinetrees, put it, 'You do feel cross, someone taking your vote and all for nothing, except that they don't do it for nothing, they do it for their own ends.' She had signed her postal vote form in all good faith and no, when Mrs Powell came to see her, she had never said what party she represented.

Interviewed about the Pinetrees voters, Mrs Powell was adamant that all had been above board. She had merely been trying to be helpful to those too elderly and frail to make it easily to the polling station. Asked if she did not think it odd that keen Labour and Liberal Democrat voters appeared to have asked her to find a Conservative to vote for them, she replied that these had been 'personal' votes for her, and those who had signed had wanted her to be their local Councillor.

So to Glencoe. Mrs Nanny Bergen had been so keen to vote that she had had herself pushed down to the polling station in her wheelchair quite early on the morning of the general election, only to be told that she had already been voted for by proxy. Nor was she alone. Her disabled daughter, Mrs Sybil Ivey, who had had a postal vote since 1969, also found she had been assigned a proxy. When her postal vote failed to appear, Mrs Ivey rang the electoral office and was told she had changed over to a proxy vote. She insisted on speaking to the Returning Officer and 'I was told I'd authorised a Mrs Stevens to vote for me.' The details on the form had been filled out by Mrs Powell. Enraged, Mrs Ivey wrote to Mrs Stevens asking her when she had given her authorisation and how Mrs Stevens had cast her vote: 'How did I vote? What's going on?' She received no reply.

As disquiet over the proxy votes continued to grow, a Mr Jimmy Walsh came forward to give interviews to both local and national television. Mr Walsh, a former driver for Mrs Powell, said that she had asked him to collect proxy votes as part of his duties from the disabled or elderly people he took in the cab. She told him she needed a lot of them and that he should give them 'a bit of patter' to get them to sign. Did they realise what they were signing? No, Mr Walsh didn't think they did. He just slapped down the form, they signed front and back, and then he stuck them up behind his sun visor and delivered them to Mrs Powell at the end of the day. How many? Probably two or three a day in the run-up to the elections, possibly as many as forty in all. Billy and Charlotte Clements, taxi-users tracked down by *Newsnight*, had thought they were signing a form to keep taxi fares down. However, as they had been determined to vote early and had turned up at their polling station before their proxy, they were able to vote – Labour.

Asked if he had not thought it unfair to pressurise elderly people into signing forms without being sure they knew what they were signing, Mr Walsh said, 'In the end I *knew* it was unfair, but what could I do? When you're an employee and told to do something, you must do it.'

Mrs Powell declined to give *Newsnight* an interview, but continued to talk to the local media. She had not told those signing proxy forms that they were giving their votes away indefinitely because, she claimed, she had not known this herself. None of those who had signed had been in any way pressured; in the nursing homes there had been staff there when she canvassed and taxi passengers in her taxis had been only too happy to support her.

When it became clear that the dead had voted, efforts were made to find out who had voted on their behalf. Thus it was that Harley Ingram, former Conservative District Council election candidate and property developer, found himself knocked up one day by a reporter from the *Sunday Mirror*. The deceased had done well by the Ingram family, for son Philip had voted on behalf of two dead women while his sister had also held a proxy vote for a dead person. When asked how this could be, Harley Ingram told the reporter to clear off. 'This is private property. Get out!'

The case of the fifth dead voter that came to light was that of a woman in her nineties who had been paralysed by a stroke for eighteen months before her death. The stroke had affected her right side and, being right-handed she had become virtually incapable of making herself understood. The proxy vote form, submitted in her name, was not even signed by her, the words 'on behalf of' being entered where the dead woman's signature was required.

Attention focused next on John Daniel, leader of the Conservative groups on both Cornwall County and Penwith District Councils and one of the county's main political activists. Mr Daniel, also famous for his very short fuse when questioned or criticised, had taken two of the proxy votes and was soon reduced to incoherent rage when questioned by reporters: 'There's nothing been abused, no one cheated and in politics, if the law says you can get proxy votes or postal votes, you're silly if you don't go out and get them. Some elections have been won on proxy votes and postal votes. And I'll tell you one thing, perhaps the Labour Party and

Liberal Democrats will learn from this and be a bit more diligent and try to get a few more. The trouble is Mr Phelp [the Labour candidate] lost. If he'd won, nobody would have known anything about it.'

Asked what he made of the seventeen Tippexed voting forms and the dead voters, Mr Daniel stoutly maintained this had not happened. If it had, the Returning Officer would have known. Assured that both the Returning Officer and the police were certain that it had indeed happened, he retreated into mumbling: 'I don't know anything about that.'

Several months passed, the police completed their inquiries and sent their report to the Crown Prosecution Service. More time passed. Then the CPS made its remarkable statement: 'Having considered all the evidence, the CPS has decided that in one case there is insufficient evidence in respect of any contravention of either electoral or criminal law, and in the other two cases [those of the Labour and Liberal Democrat errors mentioned earlier], that whilst election law had been clearly breached, it was not in the public interest to bring proceedings.'

Mrs Powell immediately shouted from the roof-tops that she had been completely vindicated and took out advertisements in all the local papers in which she stated, 'I am very pleased that I have been cleared of any criminal offence. I have protested my innocence ever since the first allegation was made.' She went on to claim that neither of the two cases mentioned in which the law had been breached had related to her but to Liberal Democrat and Labour vote mistakes, omitting to point out that both had been declared to the authorities at the time. She called on both parties to 'openly confirm' whether or not they had been contacted by the police and whether or not it was one of their respective activists who had been the subject of 'these election law breaches'. Mrs Powell did not take up the question of 'insufficient evidence'.

But the matter has not gone away. To this day at least a hundred people remain firmly convinced they had not intended that their voting right be signed away indefinitely, and they are not satisfied that their concerns have been properly addressed. Some elderly people may well have been forgetful or confused. Indeed, the daughter of one such old person said that her mother had been desperately confused for some years, although when she had voted, she had always voted Labour. It is impossible to prove whether or not all those pressed to sign proxy vote forms were fully informed that they were not only signing away their right to vote but handing their vote over to Conservative Party activists. Allegations of forged signatures remain. But neither the police nor the Returning Officer dispute the fact that five dead people voted and that seventeen postal vote forms were altered to proxy votes by the use of Tippex.

Within a short time of the CPS statement, Conservatives in the area let it be known that they had finally discovered that the forms had been altered by one of their party activists. He was not, however, available for interview, having been called to that great Returning Officer in the Sky almost immediately after the two elections. However, it does seem that there are those in the local party who were far from happy about what took place and one such told *Voice* that they had themselves collected proxy votes, that they had indeed been paid to do so and that they actually witnessed the forms being altered with Tippex by another party activist who is still very much alive.

Both national and local BBC television came in for a drubbing at the hands of the St Ives Conservative Association who have acted ever since the ruling of the Crown Prosecution Service as if they had been completely vindicated, all blame having been conveniently shuffled off on to a dead man. So far as the association is concerned, there has been no damage sustained from the scandal of the proxy votes.

A Hayle Councillor, Mr Robert Lello, reiterated this point, which he considered to be self-evident, at a Town Council meeting in December 1992 and was surprised to receive a telephone call from Mrs Powell warning him that one of her taxi drivers had overheard some of her supporters saying they were so angry at his comments that they might actually 'do him over'. At the next meeting of the Town Council Mr Lello publicly thanked her for informing him that her supporters were likely to do him mischief, observing that it was a pity she had not also informed the police. In May 1993 the Conservatives on Penwith Council, now the biggest party, blocked the recommendation of its Resource Committee that the Council support the police who, following their investigations, were forwarding suggestions to the Home Office which would help prevent future abuse of the proxy voting system.

Following the decision of the Crown Prosecution Service, two Home Office-appointed working groups, made up of civil servants and ex-Returning Officers, looked at the absent voting system (which covers both proxy and postal votes) and at the forms that allow either or both. Their reports, quietly released in mid-1994, suggest some tinkering with the design of the forms to make their purpose clearer, but there is no recommendation to scrap the particular form which allowed the fraud to take place. As the *Voice* editorial notes in its November 1994 edition, 'No one appears to have contemplated the possibility that proxy forms may not be necessary anyway, that the postal vote could meet all contingencies as it does, for example, in Germany.'

Voice also notes that while the Representation of the People Act allows for a questionable election result to be tested within a brief period following an election, the court costs of such a case must be borne by the party bringing the petition – and they can amount to as much as £30,000. The strict time limit and the difficulty of obtaining evidence in such a short time make a court case a risky venture.

Meanwhile, Mrs Powell still sits on Penwith Council by a majority of nine votes, although six proxy votes were cast on behalf of the dead and some further forty to fifty have since had to be withdrawn. At the time of writing, she still has twenty months of her four-year term to serve.

Further Afield

In the aftermath of the proxy votes scandal, *Voice* contacted as many other constituencies as time and lack of resources allowed, to see if there had been any similar instances elsewhere. In Abergavenny it was claimed that pensioners had been told they would lose their attendance allowances if they did not assign their vote to one Conservative activist. A Liberal Democrat in Bristol West claimed she was taught, when a Conservative, how to make the dead vote. Labour, in the same constituency, claimed there had been ten impersonations, and that pensioners in some residential homes had never received the postal votes they had claimed. None of these examples, however, had been followed up as they had been in St Ives. On the whole what came back from an admittedly not very large sample was, in most cases, a general feeling of unease.

In only two constituencies were matters taken further. In November 1994 Mr Warren, the Chairman of Brent Council's Education Committee, was cleared of proxy vote fraud after a four-day electoral court hearing, having been accused of casting a Labour vote for a Conservative candidate. Susan Horler, who is disabled by heart disease, claimed Mr Warren offered to help her get a postal vote. The Labour candidate lost by forty-six votes and when she made inquiries, she found her vote had been used as a proxy vote and cast in favour of the successful Conservative. Mrs Horler had to be taken to court in an ambulance, wearing an oxygen mask. The Electoral Court Commissioner, David Hallchurch, said she was a convincing witness but that on the day of Mr Warren's visit she had been having 'a bad day'. Because of this, it was claimed, her concentration had been affected and she had not made her wishes clear. The Commissioner therefore cleared Mr Warren of corrupt election practice and ordered the local Labour Party, who had brought the case, to pay Mr Warren's costs of £20,000.

In June 1994 the High Court ruled that Miles Parker, Edmonton Conservative Party agent, must stand trial on two charges brought against him under the Representation of the People Act. The offences were alleged to have been committed during a by-election for Enfield Council in 1992. Mr Parker was a political agent and, as anyone who has ever undertaken this task knows, it carries an enormous burden of responsibility, not least to ensure that the Representation of the People Act has not been broken.

On 2 November 1994 Nick Davies, writing in the *Guardian*, reported the outcome of the case which had been heard that September and had apparently sunk without trace. Certainly without media attention. It appears that Miles Parker was convicted by Barnet Magistrates' Court of forging votes. He had been until then on the pay-roll of the Conservative Party, was one of their most senior political agents, the former Chairman of the Greater London Conservative Agents' Association, a veteran of two general election campaigns and twenty-two local campaigns, and was an executive member of the party's national union.

The case turned on a by-election where the result, like that in the Penwith Council elections, was too tight to call. A Tory canvasser had visited the house of a couple called Penketh, asked Mrs Elaine Penketh if the party could count on her vote and had been told that the Penkeths were likely to be away on holiday on the day of the by-election. The canvasser then offered to get the Penkeths the forms necessary to apply for a postal vote. They duly arrived and the worker returned no fewer than three times to ensure that they had been filled in. But when the forms reached Mr Parker he struck out the request for postal votes, substituting a request for proxy votes. He then arranged for a Conservative Party supporter to vote on behalf of the Penkeths, which she did.

The Penkeths, however, decided not to go on holiday after all and, never having received confirmation or the forms necessary to enable them to vote by post, they turned up to vote in person. Like the St Ives voters, they were furious when they discovered someone had voted for them. At this stage they revealed that Mr Penketh was a policeman. He complained to Enfield Council, who called in the local police, who brought in Special Branch, after which Mr Parker was charged. However, when his case first reached the court, in May 1993, the Barnet magistrates threw it out.

According to Davies, this was because the magistrates had wanted to hear the case at 10 a.m., even though the prosecution had been told it would not commence until 2 p.m. The prosecution, therefore, pleaded that they could not call their witnesses until the afternoon. The magistrates refused to wait and as there were now no witnesses and so no available evidence, they dismissed the case. The fact that this decision was overturned is entirely due to the efforts of the prosecutor, James Lewis, who complained to the High Court. The case was duly put down to be heard again in September 1994.

Parker denied the charges. When the magistrates finally found him guilty his lawyer pleaded that if he had broken the law, then he had done so accidentally – this on behalf of a man who was a professional political agent. There was, said the solicitor, 'no deliberate intention to be dishonest'. He then asked for an absolute discharge. The magistrates fined Parker £750 plus £750 costs.

Davies gives a number of other instances, including one in Brighton, where Labour Party members found that some fifty new proxy voters had applied for votes in a marginal ward where the winning margin had been only thirty votes. Among the instances they turned up of proxy voters who had unknowingly voted Conservative were a married couple who had always voted Labour and had party posters displayed in their windows, an elderly man with Alzheimer's disease and a blind woman in her nineties.

At the time of writing, an Election Court in Burnley is due to hear a petition from the Labour Party where the number of proxy votes for one council seat went from six to 200. As in all the other instances, voters have complained that their votes have been stolen by proxies. In this instance, two others say they were impersonated at the poll. Interestingly, in the Burnley case, it is the Liberal Democrats who stand accused.

Chapter 6

WASTING PUBLIC MONEY

Few would disagree that the money raised from taxpayers should be spent as wisely and as economically as possible, especially where resources are scarce. Yet again and again we are presented with examples of prodigal spending which have passed through the system without hindrance. One of the very real criticisms which can be levelled at the Quangocracy is that so much of the power over the spending of taxpayers' money is held in the hands of unaccountable people. When it is not being spent by Quangos, vast sums of that money can disappear into the depths of the major spending departments such as the Ministry of Defence.

This benefits politicians and civil servants in two ways. The various bodies are left to get on with doing what is expected of them, but if anything goes wrong with the system, the relevant Minister or civil servant can shrug his or her shoulders and deny any responsibility: 'It wasn't me, guv.' There is no longer a doctrine of ministerial responsibility, for it is no longer the Minister's concern. Even when the trail leads right back to a Minister's very door or to decisions made in a specific department, blame is rarely attached to anyone; and as no one is actually personally responsible, no heads need to roll.

There are plenty of examples where taxpayers' money has been wasted without a thought, examples which rarely surface during harangues as to how precious a commodity it is. Again it has been necessary to be selective, but what comes across from the following examples is that while the losers have always been the taxpayers, there are a number of instances where a handful of lucky winners have earned substantial amounts of easy money.

Selling off the Port[1]

'Could you describe the ports that have been sold? What was their pre-privatisation position? How would they be described?'

'As trust ports.'

'Would they be described as a public asset?'

'They are very strange. They were set up, usually, under a statute, but they were not owned by anybody. It is difficult to suggest they are "a public asset" in the sense of the public owning them.'

'Who owned them if the public did not own them?'

'Nobody.'

'Why was the government allowed to sell them, then?'

'They sold themselves and the government gave them the powers to do so; but seeing that nobody owned them and that if nothing else happened and if they were sold, the purchaser would get them for nothing, the government decided to raise a levy which we have now got.'

Thus Mr Patrick Brown, Permanent Secretary at the Department of Transport, answering Michael Hall MP, of the Commons Public Accounts Committee on 4 February 1994.

Mr Hall was intrigued, he said, to discover that the money generated by the sales went back to the purchaser. 'Yes,' Mr Brown responded.

'It seemed as though we were giving them their own money back,' commented Mr Hall.

'Yes,' replied Mr Brown.

The sale of the trust ports produced both winners and losers – a handful of very happy winners and an awful lot of losers, notably those who lost their jobs and the country's taxpayers. Indeed, the PAC concludes that the way the sales of the different ports were organised, coupled with indefensible delays in collecting the levies on those sales, cost the state and the taxpayers millions of pounds.

Mr Brown agreed that the delays in collecting the levies cost the taxpayer £4.5m in lost interest alone.

Michael Hall made a pertinent point when pressing Mr Brown over the levy. 'Also in this report is the question of the £4.5m which has been lost to the taxpayer. Are you familiar with what would happen if a local authority lost £4.5m by failure to collect its rates for six months?'

Brown: I do not think that is a parallel case.

Hall: But you are familiar with what would happen in local government?

Brown: Yes, I am very familiar.

Hall: Elected members would be disqualified for failing to collect this money.

Quite so. But the lost levy interest was only a fraction of the overall financial loss in this sorry tale. Only the Port of London reached its highest expected price. Two ports went for less than the lowest expected figure.

When the sale of the trust ports was announced, the Department of Transport stated that it had four objectives for the sale: to facilitate the transfer of the ports to the private sector; to ensure that where a sale to a single buyer was intended, there should be fair and open competition; that particular regard should be given to the desirability of encouraging the disposal of all, or a substantial part, of the share capital to managers and other port employees; and to ensure that the port authorities obtained the best open market price.

The DoT obtained benchmark valuations for each port, the committee was told, in advance of sales. Questioned later as to why the sale prices obtained reached the upper limit of that benchmark in only one instance, the department replied that the benchmarks had only been put in place 'to give some feel for where the price ought to be; that by definition they could not always be accurate; and that they were only estimates and judgements of advisers, based on their experience and in view of the market at the time. Nor was the benchmark an absolute floor.'

The committee asked why Tees and Hartlepool had rejected the highest bidder for their port, £202m from Maritime Transport

Services Ltd, in favour of £180m from Teesside Holdings, and was told that the port authority justified its choice on the grounds that Teesside Holdings had promised to spend more on the infrastructure of the port.

But the worst instance was that of the port of Medway, which included the old port of Sheerness and stretched round as far as Chatham. Sold off for £29.7m, it was resold within eighteen months for £103m in circumstances which were, to say the least, highly contentious.

Not long before the port came up for sale there had been management changes and it was the new management team which decided to go for it when the chance came to purchase the port. The work force were asked to give the deal their utmost support by working at maximum efficiency and were also encouraged to become shareholders if and when the deal came through and the bid was successful. They were assured, as was the Department of Transport, that if successful, the management buy-out team would maintain their terms and conditions of service at the existing levels. Fired by what appeared to be excellent prospects, the work force did all in its power to assist in the successful bid for the port and, when it went through, many of them invested their savings in shares at £2.40 each.

MP James Couchman asked Mr Brown what the 'benchmark' had been for Medway. Between £38m and £56m, he was told. Asked to disclose what value had been ascribed by his advisers to the development of the Chatham dockyard part of the Medway port, Mr Brown replied, 'I'm afraid I cannot. I do not have that information.' Later the department provided the committee with a note to the effect that the advisers had put the value of the Chatham part of the port at £4m–£6m and that area, plus surplus land, at £9.4m.

The management buy-out triumphed after a second bidder withdrew, and champagne duly flowed in the offices. It did not, however, flow for long on the dockside. Within months the work force was cut from 668 to 260, while shares in the new company soared in value from £2.40 to £35. Not only did almost two-thirds of the work force find themselves out of a job in an area of little employment, but, to add insult to injury they were forced to sell back their shares to the company for £2.50, a profit of just 10p, when the market value was fourteen times that. Eighteen months after its successful bid, the management buy-out team gleefully sold off the port for £103m, thus making a profit of over £73m and turning its Chief Executive into a millionaire.

James Couchman suggested to Mr Brown that the reduction in the work force in 1992 was 'quite brutal. It is resented around my constituency.' 'It was a significant reduction,' Mr Brown replied. As to those remaining being offered a new contract with substantially worse conditions, Mr Brown knew nothing of this. 'That is a matter for the port, not the government.' He only knew of the sale of employees' shares and the rock-bottom price 'from the papers', but regarding the company, 'the reduction in the work force will have made a significant difference to its profitability'. Asked if it was true that the shares were not reissued after the forced purchase from the work force, but kept by the management, Mr Brown responded, 'I have no idea.' Pressed further, that if this was the case, only a handful of those with shares actually benefited from the sale, Mr Brown agreed that might be so. 'Are you comfortable with that?' James Couchman persisted. Said Mr Brown: 'What happens in a private sector business is not a matter with which the Department of Transport is concerned. It is a matter between the individual shareholders and the company.'

It was also revealed that when the management had applied to buy Medway in the first place, they had stated that they were going to maintain their terms and conditions of service at the existing level. 'I understand the management said, "We're here to stay,"' said James Couchman. 'What they did not do was put in brackets: but not for very long. Should there have been undertakings given which were binding? Should there be such undertakings in the future and should you in fact avoid the sort of trade sale which has happened from this management buy-out at a very substantial profit?'

The response was that one of the problems of selling on to the private sector was that, in the cold light of day of market movements, a management may well be required to take steps to improve the efficiency of the business. It was difficult to see how any such undertaking could be made binding. Asked whether or not advice with regard to the purchase of shares should not have been given to the work force, Mr Brown replied that the department did not believe it had ever been part of its remit to give advice to individuals as to whether or not they should subscribe to a management buy-out. They had a free choice.

The committee was rightly highly critical of the Medway sale, noting that the taxpayer had received a mere £29.7m, while the buy-out team had grossed over £103m. It particularly noted that the key factor in making the port so tempting to another buyer was that the work force, which had worked so hard to maintain the port's excellent turnover, had been drastically reduced in the run-up to the sale. 'In all these circumstances we are surprised at the department's view that they had not done badly for the taxpayer in this sale.'

All in all the PAC concluded it was far from satisfied with the way the port sales had been handled. With regard to the delay in collecting the levy, its report states, 'We note this delay arose partly because of disputes with two ports about whether or not expenditure of no more than £1.6m was deductible in calculating the amount of the levy they had to pay, and partly because of uncertainty over the recoverability of VAT on certain items. We are also concerned that the eventual settlement resulted in the recovery of no more than £300,000 of the disputed £1.6m at a cost to the taxpayer of £4.5m.'

'What a Swell Party That Was . . .'

Every now and then light is shone into the Augean stables of the Ministry of Defence and the waste that has continued even in this new era of huge cut-backs and the so-called peace dividend. Again and again the taxpayer has lost out, from serious incidents of straightforward fraud which have gone undetected for years to incidents bordering on farce. In 1994 two ex-MoD officials received jail sentences.

On 24 May Bernard Trevelyan, who had headed the Ministry's

Light Armoured Engineering Systems Department, was jailed for a year. He had pocketed thousands of pounds in arms contract backhanders and had used a front company to leak technical and financial secrets on valuable orders. He was found guilty at Southwark Crown Court on four charges of corruption involving a total of £8,652, and one of attempted corruption which would have brought him a further £28,580. Also before the court was David Oliver, Managing Director of defence agents Imvec, fined £4,000 after being found guilty of paying his friend, Mr Trevelyan, a backhander of £2,000 for a report on armoured vehicles.[2]

Judge Michael Harris had been told that Mr Trevelyan had 'a great deal of influence' over who won contracts for armoured car equipment and machine-gun mountings and had set up a sham company, Surrey Consultants, which he used as a secret pipeline to receive up to £5,500 a time in return for his influence in granting MoD contracts. He had wanted, said the judge, 'a slice of the action'. 'However we take pride,' continued the judge a trifle optimistically, 'that the public service in this country is largely free of corruption.'[3]

Two days later Gordon Foxley was jailed for four years after being paid £1.3m in kickbacks by foreign arms companies and a further £1m from other sources, in what was described as Britain's biggest cash corruption case. While it might well be understandable that Mr Trevelyan was able to conceal shady dealing concerning a few thousand pounds, peanuts in MoD terms, it beggars belief that Foxley got away with what he did for years without anyone suspecting anything was wrong. No one apparently thought it was odd that an MoD official, a director of the Ministry's Munitions Procurement Department on a salary of around £30,000 a year, should live in a £450,000 Edwardian mansion at Henley-on-Thames; that he should own a clutch of other expensive properties and be able to buy another mansion, costing £345,000, to give to his son; that he should have a whole fleet of expensive cars, one with the custom-acquired numberplate SLY 3; and that banks had happily allowed him to take out large loans on behalf of members of his family. The scam had gone on for years, from 1979 until 1984, when he retired from the MoD. After he had finally been caught, armaments firms from Germany,

Italy and Norway queued up to say how easily and openly they had obtained MoD contracts via Foxley in exchange for cash.[4]

While commenting that Foxley had 'planned and executed this fraud with meticulous care' and had covered himself 'every step, every inch of the way to avoid detection', Judge Andrew Brook still managed to find mitigating circumstances for not passing a maximum sentence. These included Foxley's age (sixty-nine), his health, 'and the fact that he had played an important part in keeping the armed forces supplied during the Falklands War'. The judge estimated that, after taking inflation into account, Foxley had only benefited from his crimes to the tune of £2,092,500. He also decided that while much of Foxley's property would be seized, he could retain his £450,000 riverside mansion.[5]

Foxley's son, Paul, an unqualified accountant, was jailed for six months for burning incriminating Swiss bank account statements during the police investigations into his father's affairs. The MoD has admitted that some of Foxley's assets stashed away in Swiss bank accounts may never be recovered.

Judge Brook also stated that he did not think Mr Foxley's behaviour had caused his former employers 'any actual loss or damage', nor was he satisfied that there was sufficient evidence before him that he had caused any jobs to be lost. This is disputed by the sacked workers from the Royal Ordnance factory in Blackburn, Lancashire, who claim that 1,000 of them lost their jobs after the contracts it was fully expected would come to them went abroad to Foxley's paymasters. Commenting afterwards, Jack Dromey, National Secretary of the Transport and General Workers' Union said, 'Repeated representations were made by dismayed managers and workers at the loss of contracts to inferior competition, often charging the MoD more. The MoD spurned these representations and simply said that "value for money" meant that the orders would go abroad. Nothing was untoward, the Ministry said, yet it was known that Foxley was leading a lavish lifestyle, way beyond his means. He was an obscene product of his times. An inquiry is necessary to ensure that never again is the public ripped off in this way.'[6]

Shadow Environment spokesman Jack Straw commented that Foxley's sentence was 'further evidence of how soft judges can be on white-collar fraud. If Foxley had robbed a bank of £1.5m he would have received at least ten years.'

On 16 October 1994 the *Observer* published details of a confidential report on Foxley which had come into its hands. The ten-page analysis puts the final reckoning for the Grade 6 civil servant, who – the paper reminds its readers – was on £25,000 a year when he retired, at between £100m and £130m. Detailed research into the bribes accepted by Foxley in his capacity as head of the MoD's ammunition procurement branch, particularly regarding German involvement, 'demolish the notion that Foxley's was a victimless crime'.

The account includes:

'Up to 300 jobs lost at the Royal Ordnance factory in Blackburn, Lancashire, which failed to win the orders that went to the firms that gave him backhanders. Cost: £2.1m a year to the taxpayer in unemployment benefits.

'Royal Ordnance, Blackburn, went from making a profit to making a loss, largely due to the rundown caused by Mr Foxley preferring foreign suppliers. When Royal Ordnance was privatised, his activities had wiped £35m off the sale price. Cost: £13.75m of lost contracts for Royal Ordnance, now part of British Aerospace, plus redundancy payments of up to £12,000 a worker, or £3.6m in total.

'As the work dried up, much of the factory's machinery and equipment was dumped in skips. Skills, developed over years, were destroyed. Cost of replacement and retraining: £24m.

'Originally the MoD was being supplied with a Royal Ordnance fuse costing £6 each. Mr Foxley persuaded the Army to take the German Jughans DM111A fuse at £14.40m. Cost: £12.9m, being the excess paid by the MoD on the Jughans contract.

'In the case of Borletti, an Italian company that bribed Foxley, the entire contract was a waste. The Italian fuse did not work in the rain and was ineffective in practice and battle conditions. Cost: £15m to the British taxpayer.'

The police, it seems, have been unable to put a figure on the cost of inquiries which took them to banks and properties in Switzerland, the Channel Isles and the Isle of Man as well as to foreign companies from which Foxley received bribes.

Cost overruns are also a regular part of life at the MoD. No one, during the whole furore over the further defence cut-backs in 1994, mentioned the one thing above all else which has proved devastatingly expensive, the Trident programme. We now have a fleet of expensive submarines armed with enormous nuclear firepower targeted at – what? In July a report from the Auditor General[7] stated that the MoD had wasted £8bn on building facilities for Trident. It revealed huge financial overruns which, it said, were caused by delays, mismanagement, lack of communication and design faults, including 'a failure to appreciate the cost of protecting the public from nuclear accidents'; the last is staggering in view of the mountains of literature and expertise on this very subject which is easily available to anyone. All together Trident is now 72 per cent over budget, the facilities likely to cost £1.9bn instead of the £1.1bn estimated; the programme itself is anything up to two and a half years late; and the cost of the 'consultants' who have presided over the shambles has risen almost 200 per cent, from £122m to £360m, almost 20 per cent of the total cost of providing the facilities.

From the outset, claimed the Auditor General, the MoD and the former Property Services Agency did not have either the level of control or the expertise necessary to communicate their requirements or monitor the project's progress. The worst example is a ship-lift as high as an eleven-storey building and as long as Wembley Stadium which can pull a 16,000-tonne submarine clear of the water. The contract for it, awarded to those doughty financial contributors to Conservative Party funds, Trafalgar House, is two and a half years late, the cost has risen from £100m to £314m and design changes have required 7,200 alterations. It has still not passed all its safety tests. Among many setbacks was a failure to realise it was being built in an area of high asbestos contamination. Another huge cost overrun was involved in the building of access roads by Tarmac Construction Ltd. These were completed seventeen months late, with an increase from £61m to £115m, due to a failure to survey the route of the road properly.

The list goes on and on, and Labour and Liberal Democrat MPs were said to be furious because of a government decision that the Auditor General's report should be published immediately after

Parliament went into recess, thus ensuring it would receive little publicity and there would be no chance to question what had happened, something which has become increasingly commonplace.

However, enough of this financial megawastage and on to party time, the twenty-fifth anniversary of the Royal Naval Supply and Transport Service to be precise. According to the Public Accounts Committee's report on MoD irregular expenditure, this junket took place in 1992 and no expense seems to have been spared. Social security claimants creeping down to their local offices in the hope of a hardship loan will, no doubt, be delighted to know that tens of thousands of pounds of taxpayers' money went on ensuring that senior MoD staff had a good time at the thrash. Two ships were hired, the *Sir Galahad* in Rosyth and the *Argus* off Portsmouth. The *Argus* party alone cost £79,000. Reporting on the event in the House of Commons on 25 October 1993, PAC Chairman Robert Sheldon MP commented, 'It must have been quite a party.' He was asked to give way by MP Michael Shersby who enquired, 'Will the Right Honourable Gentleman refresh the memory of those members of the committee who are here today as to the cost of floodlighting the party? I seem to recall that it was about £28,000 for a *non-night* party.' Mr Sheldon replied, 'My Honourable Friend is just about right.' Other expenses included a chauffeur-driven car at a cost of £76 to transport a guest from Edinburgh to Rosyth to attend the *Galahad* party, and expensive overnight hotel accommodation for those attending the parties in both ports.[8]

It is a rare occurrence for any Commons report to cause one to laugh out loud, but the questioning of the senior civil servant Christopher Frances, KCB, Permanent Under-Secretary of State at the MoD, and his responses in civil service mandarin-speak could be lifted straight off the page and into *Yes, Minister*.[9] MP Kim Howells asked if there were no ballrooms or other venues suitable for such a party, rather than hiring two ships. Sir Christopher replied that he was sure there were but this was a very special occasion. 'You would not expect the RAF to hold it [the event] in a jumbo jet?' persisted Mr Howells. No, Sir Christopher would not, but he might well expect them to hold it in a hangar 'particularly if there were airmen unfamiliar with airfields as there are some members of the RNSTS who are unfamiliar with being aboard ship. This was seen as an opportunity to give them that experience.' Questioned as to the amount the party cost, Sir Christopher responded that it was a minute percentage of the Defence budget. 'Just small change?' asked MP James Couchman. He continued, 'In terms of these old naval traditions of rum, sodomy and the lash, the *Argus* appears to have opted for rum, is that right, in generous measure?' Sir Christopher did not think there had been all that much rum.

Mr Couchman: It must have been quite grand. £5,000 on prizes and gifts. Was that looked at?

Sir Christopher: Yes.

Mr Couchman: Was that a present for each of those attending or spot prizes or what?

Sir Christopher: I have no idea what led to the presentation of gifts, but it would have been that kind of thing.

Mr Couchman: In terms of the provision of music, it cost ten times as much to have a band or whatever on the *Argus* as the *Sir Galahad*. My local Mayor had Joe Loss last Friday night at £2,500. Did the *Argus* have Joe Loss?

Sir Christopher: I am afraid I do not know who the *Argus* had.

It was, as Chairman Robert Sheldon said, quite a party. One might add the chorus line of that number from the popular musical *High Society* – 'What a swell party that was!'

The same report also picked out further irregular expenditure, from the purchase of a coach and minibuses for social trips at a cost of £628,000 to £17,586 on 'staff amenities', including go-karts, £6,000 on a smart caravan and £480 on commemorative glasses for MoD staff. There was also the £9.4m on a staff incentive scheme which operated for only one year. All together the minor irregular expenditure on 'novel or contentious items' came to £1,076,422.

Sir Christopher was questioned closely as to whether or not heads would roll as a result of what had happened. He agreed that this sum had been improperly spent and that faults ran from top to bottom of the system; he denied that had he said, as was claimed, that no one had been to blame, it was 'another way of saying that a great many people were to blame in different degrees

. . . we have a sort of spectrum here.' Had heads rolled, were senior officials rebuked? A senior civil servant and a line manager had been rebuked. Such a person would be in the last couple of hundred people in seniority. But no one higher up? Had any of those at the very top been rebuked? 'No, they have not but I do want to say that the people of whom I speak are on any reckoning very senior people.' But they were not the people at the real top, not the top twenty, top ten. Sir Christopher had blamed the guidelines; who had issued them? 'The guidance was issued from the group that manages the finance chaired by my predecessor.' But surely there would have been other people there as well as the Chairman, including senior finance officers? Sir Christopher agreed there would. 'Have any of them been rebuked?' 'No.' This was because the responsibility had been spread throughout the system.

In their conclusions the committee noted that they had asked the MoD just how much money would have to be misspent to justify disciplinary action. 'They told us that in their view it was more a question of the circumstances in which the misspending took place. In this case there had been no indication of fraud or personal gain. Misspending had arisen from professional misjudgement over the application of the guidance.' There could be circumstances which might lead to formal disciplinary proceedings, but none of the examples fell into this category. The committee were far from satisfied. The whole farrago had revealed an unacceptable failure by civil servants and a predisposition to excuse poor standards at senior level. It particularly noted 'that the Department decided not to seek to recover the irregular expenditure because of the administrative complications and the possible effects on further efforts to increase efficiency. We consider that where possible the Department should have requested all staff involved to repay the benefits they had received from irregular expenditure.'

Among past 'irregularities' uncovered by the National Audit Office and the PAC was the theft of assets, including the loss of £500,000's worth of office and computer equipment in 1990–91 and tens of thousands of pounds in fraudulent claims for travel and subsistence. This latter amounted to 283 proven cases of fraud. In October 1992 Robert Sheldon had told the House, 'Nevertheless we found that only 45 per cent of those guilty of fraud were dismissed. Could 55 per cent of them claim exceptional circumstances? We find it hard to reconcile the dismissal policy with the number of exceptions to it, now running at 55 per cent.'[10]

Even the jolly parties paled into insignificance, however, beside what was unintentionally revealed to Labour MP Stephen Byers when he tabled questions about remuneration for top servicemen. The answers revealed that the top seventy-seven lucky men are living what can only be described as millionaire lifestyles in houses worth around £500,000 each, paid for out of taxpayers' money and run at our expense. Individual furniture bills and wages for domestic staff add to the £5m subsidy these people receive from the taxpayer, according to the *Guardian* (1.8.94), to whom Mr Byers passed on the information. Apparently we have all paid for such essential items for the defence of the realm as five dog kennels at a cost of £50,000; £25,000 on a 'his and hers' garage for one commmanding officer; £55,000 on a commodore's furniture; and £500,000 on a NATO field marshal's house which had cost £2m to buy. The whole scandal surfaced because a House of Commons Table Office clerk misread Byers' handwriting and gave him information for which he had not actually asked! Hitherto, Ministers had refused to answer such questions for, as they put it, 'security reasons'.

Top spender is Admiral Sir Michael Layard with a salary of £100,000, a £500,000 home, on which £63,000 was spent in 1993, plus £2,500 on furniture and £173,000 on general household finances. The domestic staff bill alone for Admiral Sir Hugo White, Commander in Chief of the Fleet, was £157,000, plus a £63,000 home 'maintenance' bill and £16,000 on furniture. Naval cut-backs have hit Plymouth and Devonport hard, while the work force in the dockyard has, in recent years, been slashed by two-thirds. Keyham ward, closest to the dockyard gates, is, by the government's own figures, one of the most deprived areas in the whole country. Yet Admiral Sir Roy Newman, based in Plymouth, has a £500,000 house on which some £80,700 has been spent during the last two years, along with £24,000 on furniture. His domestic staff budget is £142,000. Even the lower-ranking Commodore Michael Johnson, in charge of the Drake base at Devonport, spent £55,000 on furnishing his base house, eleven times more than his opposite number in Rosyth. The list goes on and on. The commanding officer of Dartmouth Naval College, Captain Simon Moore, was the lucky winner of the five dog kennels and the 'his and hers' garage.

The Ministry of Defence, defending the spending to the *Guardian*, stated that 'many of the residences are part of the national heritage and are listed buildings which need a lot of expensive maintenance'. Also, these posts carry 'onerous responsibilities for entertaining', such as holding regimental dinners and entertaining foreign guests. And, presumably, parties. So that's all right then.

Efficiency Savings, Ministerial Style

In April 1994 the Cabinet Office revealed, after much prodding from Labour MP Alan Milburn, that Ministers had spent £565m of taxpayers' money on management consultants brought in to bring about efficiency savings.[11] This had resulted in savings of – £10m! Commenting on this during an angry exchange of questions at Prime Minister's Question Time, the late Leader of the Opposition, John Smith, remarked that taxpayers, currently facing major tax increases, would 'bitterly resent this further example of this government's now legendary incompetence'. Mr Major described this attack as 'bogus'.

Not all Ministers had been prepared to release details of their expenditure on consultancies for efficiency savings because, they said, the information was 'too expensive to collect'. Jonathan Aitken, then Defence Procurement Minister, Michael Forsyth, then junior at Employment, Tony Baldry, junior Environment Minister, and Alastair Goodlad at the Foreign Office had all refused to respond to requests for enlightenment as to the costs of their efficiency drive, yet, when the Cabinet Report was finally published, three of them were among the top seven spenders.

Figures available for 1992–93 show that the Ministry of Transport spent £197,924,700 on 111 contracts for efficiency savings, Social Security £100,900,000 on 1,025 contracts, the Department of Trade and Industry £29,369,000 on 402 contracts. The Department of Health spent over £18m but would not specify the number of contracts, the Northern Ireland Office over £16m on 1,349, the Cabinet Office itself in 1993–94 over £7.5m, the number of contracts not being available; the Department of Agriculture over £7m on 111, the Treasury just under £6m on eighty-two, and the Home Office nearly £3.5m on seventy, the last two figures referring to the financial year 1993–94.

In August 1994 it was learned that the government has spent £258m on advice from consultants on its privatisation programme since Margaret Thatcher launched the initiative in 1980. The Department of Transport, which privatised British Airways and the National Bus Company, topped the league at £107m. Other big spenders include the Department of Trade at £67.6m for advice on selling off British Telecom and Cable and Wireless, and the Department of the Environment at £26m, which includes the bill for selling off the Property Services Agency. These figures were released in a series of written parliamentary answers to Labour MP Alan Milburn. The Ministry of Defence had released information to the effect that it had spent just £2m in 1993 on advice on selling off the dockyards at Devonport and Rosyth, but a Cabinet Office report released in early August revealed it had actually spent £259m, which included payments to consultants specialising in market testing and computer systems.

On 5 August 1994 Labour's Transport spokesman, Frank Dobson, showed that the government had spent £16.8m on assorted consultants for advice on rail privatisation, more than three times the £5m it would have cost to settle the 1994 rail strike. He listed twelve companies which had been retained by the Department of Transport to advise on aspects of the sell-off, including City solicitors Linklaters and Paines, who had, to that date, been paid £6m for legal advice. Accountants Cooper and Lybrand and Putnam Hayes and Barlett received £2.5m between them for advice on access charging. According to Rebecca Smithers, the *Guardian*'s transport correspondent, Coopers and Lybrand twice reported back to the government that it was unable to devise a suitable regime, before coming up with the controversial formula that effectively doubles the price of access to the track. Defending the expenditure, a spokeswoman for the Ministry of Transport said (5.8.94), 'Ministers believe this money is well spent because privatisation will lead to a more efficient railway that will be less of a burden on the taxpayer.'

The Great Training Scam

Back in 1992 the PAC expressed some concern over the government's youth training programme, stating the need for improved financial control over training expenditure 'if overpayments are to be prevented and fraud and corruption deterred'. Some £6m had been disbursed in overpayments, many Training and Enterprise Councils (TECs) had received large sums of money when trainees had been absent from training programmes without authority and some Councils had obtained funding by stretching the training programmes beyond their intentions. 'The amounts involved were significant.' The committee had then been informed that the tightening of financial controls was to be made 'the top priority'.

Not so, it would seem. In April 1994 the media were flooded with reports of financial mismanagement over a range of training and job schemes. Allegations included government-backed job clubs being paid to find work for their members lasting only one day and these temporary postings counting towards the contractual targets agreed between the Department of Employment and the clubs.[12] Those who ponder on the government employment statistics and how these tally with what seems to be the position in the real world might be interested to know that one-day placements are included in the government's employment statistics. In 1991–92 the government boasted that there was a 56 per cent success rate for members of job clubs finding work. John Prescott, then Labour's Employment spokesman, inquired how it was possible for a job lasting one day to be justified as any sort of success, especially as job clubs were limited to those who had been out of work for at least six months. He suspected collusion between the government and employers to provide short-term temporary work in order to massage the unemployment statistics.

There are 1,450 job clubs with an annual membership of 250,000. Most are now privately run and financed by the government under a scheme for payment by results. In 1993 they received £60m in government funding. In March 1994 the Department of Employment had written to club leaders in the south-west London area saying that 'any placing of a day or more can be counted, and this has been the case since April 1993'. Offices which had not been following this rule could now count placings retrospectively. Questioned by the *Independent*, a Department of Employment spokesperson confirmed that a club would be entitled to a payment for finding jobs lasting a day.[13]

This came hard on the heels of a report that one of the biggest employment training companies, the government-sponsored JHP, had faked City and Guilds RSA certificates at its West Cumbria office in order to obtain extra government cash. This came to light after investigations carried out by Labour MP Dale Campbell-Savours.[14]

On 21 April 1994 junior Employment Minister Ann Widdicombe announced that the department's internal audit service was to investigate JHP Training following disclosures that the company had obtained cash from the government based on bogus claims. This came amid further allegations of private training firms pocketing tens of thousands of pounds of taxpayers' money by claiming qualifications gained by phantom trainees. Dale Campbell-Savours told the House that he had found certificates awarded to people who had never attended such courses and did not even know they had been awarded them.

JHP admitted that the fraud had taken place but claimed that it had involved 'former employees'. The firm offered to return £10,000 to the Cumbria Training and Enterprise Council, but this was rejected. Hugh Pitman, Chairman of JHP, then went on to complain that the MP had obtained documents from former employees. This particular fraud followed the privatisation of all training courses for eighteen to twenty-five-year-olds. Under the new scheme TECS have to appoint private firms as training agents. For every trainee awarded a certificate, the company receives between £250 and £750. Speaking in the House, Mr Campbell-Savours claimed that investigations into JHP would 'reveal the extensive forgery of trainer and trainee signatures, the theft of public money, the submission of falsified documents and attendance records to TEC officials, unreasonable pressure having been exerted on employees, and the deliberate misleading of national examination boards'. He said he wanted an inquiry by the National Audit Office and the Public Accounts Committee to look into the whole question, not 'a private audit inquiry reporting to a minister'.

In May under the heading 'Second Training Scam Alleged' the *Guardian* reported that JHP Training was facing another set of allegations involving phantom students. The new allegation concerned the company's Barrow office, leading to the tabling of a Commons motion by Dale Campbell-Savours and fellow MP John Hutton. The motion named a young man, Paul Hamilton, who works in a furnishing shop and for whom money was claimed for a course he had never attended. The motion says that JHP 'fraudulently produced an assessment sheet falsifying information as to training that did not take place'. Efforts had then been made to pursue Paul Hamilton's employers for signatures on time sheets. Questioned about the allegation, Hugh Pitman confirmed that two members of staff had approached Mr Hamilton and his employers and produced paperwork for assessment for a NVQ course. But he denied that they had produced assessment information on Mr Hamilton fraudulently. The discrepancy had arisen because Mr Hamilton and his employers had once considered that he might take the course but had decided not to proceed. The inquiry continues.

The above are just a handful of examples from the Departments of Transport, Defence and Employment, the Cabinet Office and the privatised and unaccountable Quangos, agencies and companies which now undertake the tasks that used to be the responsibility of Ministers and ministerial departments. There are plenty more, right across the board.[15]

Chapter 7

THE GRAVY TRAIN

'It is justified by what the non-executive directors of the board think I am worth.' Thus Sir Desmond Pitcher, Chairman of North West Water, defending a salary of £338,000 plus £200,000 in shares.[1] It is hardly surprising that his non-executive directors and shareholders are pretty happy in view of the money the water consumers of the North West are pouring into their bank accounts, nor that they will back Sir Desmond all the way and pay him in telephone number figures so long as the gravy train keeps going.

Sir Desmond typifies with startling clarity the great divide between those who are constantly exhorted to tighten their belts for the public good and those who feel they are so uniquely qualified to hold their particular posts that the sky is the limit where their own salaries are concerned.

Outside that cosy world, we learn that the poorest 10 per cent of the population are no better off than they were twenty-seven years ago and that there have been record increases in inequality over the last fifteen years despite a 50 per cent rise in average incomes and a doubling in the income of the richest 10 per cent over the same period. Eleven million people were estimated to be living under a poverty line of half the national average income in 1991, compared with three million living below the same threshold in 1977. The income share of the poorest tenth has fallen from 4.2 per cent of the national average in 1961 to 3.0 per cent in 1991, while the income share of the wealthiest has risen from 22 per cent to 25 per cent over the same period. The proportion of families with children in the poorest 10 per cent has increased from a third in 1961 to more than half.

Looking at income distribution, the poorest 5 per cent of the population saw their real income fall in absolute terms between 1979 and 1991, before taking account of housing costs, while the richest 5 per cent found their incomes rose by 58 per cent.[2] The very poorest, who used to be able to get loans from the Department of Social Security for essential pieces of equipment, cookers, beds, etc, now have to plead instead for loans, which may be refused either because the Social Fund has run out of money or because, almost unbelievably, the applicant is considered too poor to be able to pay the loan back and so must go without even the means to cook hot food.

Meanwhile the exhortations continue. Michael Portillo, when still a Treasury Minister, announced in May 1994 that there was to be a new 'benefit crackdown'. Aware of the spiralling cost of housing benefit paid to the poorest families, he proposed a plan which would force them into more 'appropriate accommodation'. Cut-backs in housing benefit, coupled with the refusal to allow local authorities to spend the money gained from selling off housing stock to build more low-rental accommodation, will only result, as opponents of the plan point out, in even more homeless people on the streets adding to those 'eyesores' John Major finds so obnoxious.[3]

The prolonged strike of railway signal workers in the summer of 1994 came about in no small part because the government, as it finally admitted, intervened in the negotiations between Railtrack and the signalmen. The signalmen wanted a rise of 11 per cent in recognition of increased productivity and substantial redundancies. Railtrack apparently offered 5.7 per cent and it is almost certain that this would have been accepted. But the government vetoed the deal because the Treasury had decided that the amount paid to public sector workers must not exceed 2.5 per cent.[4] Any deviation would, the argument goes, only encourage other workers, like Oliver Twist, to ask for more.

These facts need to be registered when we examine the remuneration of those who have jumped aboard the gravy train. The latest analysis of directors' pay undertaken by Labour Research shows a healthy growth in salaries of 19.2 per cent per annum, in spite of inflation rising at less than 3 per cent. The man topping the pay-rise league is none other then the elusive Octav Botnar. As has already been mentioned, Mr Botnar, a major donator of funds to the Conservative Party, is wanted for questioning in this country by the authorities on tax fraud charges. The fugitive director of the motor dealer group Automotive Financial and of Nissan UK, currently in Switzerland, has had his pay increased by 2,830 per cent. Perhaps that should also be put in words – two thousand, eight hundred and thirty per cent. The runner-up to Mr Botnar is Derek Hunt of the furniture group MFI with a pay rise of a mere 604 per cent, bringing his salary, including management and performance-related bonuses, to £1,634,000 per annum.[5]

Nor should we forget the world of entertainment. Theatrical entrepreneur Cameron Mackintosh was paying himself £9,732,065 a year as at October 1993, a pay rise of 17 per cent on 1992. He was also paid a further £1,020,429 in pension contributions.[6]

Huge salaries are not the end of the matter. Many top company executives have substantial share stakes in their companies which, as well as providing them with dividends, are conveniently non-taxable. Indeed some of them see the dividends from shares as their main source of income. Labour Research, examining the shareholdings of big dividend earners, discovered seventy-eight directors earning over £500,000 a year from this source alone. 'Between them,' says its report, Directorships Pay Rich Dividends,[7] 'these seventy-eight received a staggering total dividend income of £166,538,410. Among them were thirty-two directors who earned £1m or more, including four who earned at least £14m a year, or £269,230 a week.' Topping the league at the end of 1993 was Conrad Black of the Telegraph group with £19.2m in dividends, although this is likely to drop in 1994 due to the broadsheets' price war. Andrew Lloyd Webber, on a salary of £1.1m from his Really Useful Theatre group, earned far more from dividends in the company – a really useful £15.07m. David Sainsbury of the Sainsbury supermarket chain earned £14.5m in dividends in the form of shares (over the years Sainsburys has given its shareholders the option of receiving their dividends in the form of more shares).

Four directors of Lloyds of London brokers Benfield appear, ranging from Matthew Harding's £2.32m down to David Colman's £906,250. As Harding's salary as at August 1993 was £2.28m, his total income for the year was £4.6m. The report points out that directors can also make huge sums by selling off some of their shares on the stock market, citing Robert Gavron, Chairman of the printers St Ives, who made £6,382,041 on the sale of 2.7 million company shares; Sir Bernard Ashley of Laura Ashley, who made £7.85m on a share sale; and Richard Biffa of the waste disposal group Shanks and McEwan, who sold a million shares for £2.23m.

Indeed shareholders, unlike employees, appear to have survived the last recession rather well, even when company profits were falling and staff were being laid off. An analysis of ninety-eight out of the hundred companies listed in the FTSE 100, or 'Footsie' as it is known, showed that sixty-seven companies (68 per cent of the total) increased their dividend pay-outs by more than their companies' rise in profits throughout the entire period. In fact thirty-eight of the companies increased dividends even though profits had actually fallen. Of these Vodafone saw dividends rise by nearly twice the rate of increase in profits, while the Carlton Communications Group saw dividends soar by 80 per cent while profits fell by 9 per cent. Among companies whose incomes moved from profit to loss during the recession, ICI maintained its dividend levels, while General Accident and Sun Alliance actually raised their dividends by 7 per cent and 14 per cent respectively. Labour Research puts this down to companies trying to placate their big institutional shareholders.

Meanwhile staff losses continued, a notable case in point being British Telecom with drastic cut-backs. In spite of this, profits in 1992 fell by 14.3 per cent, while shareholders' dividends rose by 32.2 per cent. 'Clearly,' says Labour Research, 'the wealth of shareholders is considered more crucial by the corporate world than the basic right of workers to earn a living.'[8]

Generous redundancy pay-outs are rarely made to ordinary workers, however hard and loyally they might have served their companies; not so with executives. Here it is hello to the golden goodbye. The term varies – golden goodbye, golden handshake, golden farewell, golden parachutes are all frequently used; the operative word is 'golden'. During 1992–93 forty-eight directors each received £100,000 or more in golden goodbyes, totalling £17,276,478. Eleven received over half a million, two of whom wheeled away over £1m. Labour Research points out that the number of directors actually receiving such mega pay-offs is larger than this as companies are not legally required to detail individual pay-outs and, in many cases, only give a total pay-off figure and the number of directors involved.

Topping the bill is none other than Robert Horton, now of Railtrack, with his pay-off from British Petroleum of £1.5m. Runner-up is Ronald Groom of Biltons, the builders, paid £1,067,500 when he stood down as Chief Executive while remaining on the company pay-roll as a non-executive director. Michael Montague, who had headed the lock and heater firm Yale and Valor, was paid £892,000 when he left after the firm had been taken over by Williams Holdings. Don McCrickard, Chief Executive of the TSB, the bank privatised during the Thatcher years and the bank 'that likes to say yes', left suddenly in August 1992. He then said 'yes' to a golden goodbye of £763,432. Fifth in the line of mega pay-offs is Gene Lockhart of the Midland Bank who got £735,658 following its takeover by the Bank of Hong Kong and Shanghai. Fellow Midland executive George Loudun received £720,000.[9]

Even if an executive is actually sacked or encouraged to leave following policy failures, many soon find seats on other boards. James Kerr Muir, who left Tate and Lyle in 1991 with a golden goodbye of £500,000, became Finance Director of the Kingfisher Group in 1992, while David Hankinson, who resigned from Lucas Industries in February 1992 with a golden goodbye of £352,000, joined baker giant Rank Hovis McDougall on a five-year contract worth £160,000 a year. In April 1993, following a takeover of his new company, Hankinson was again out of a job but received, according to Labour Research, a golden pay-off in the region of £800,000.

The reason for the mega pay-offs is that top executives currently enjoy long-term rolling contracts running usually for three to five years, so if a company wants to sack one of them or force him to resign, it has to pay out the whole unfinished part of the contract.

The Privatised Trough

But it is the fortunate few at the top of the privatised utilities whose progress on the gravy train has caused most public fury. A few examples of going rates in the electricity companies paint a general picture as at August 1994:

- Southern Electricity Chief Executive Henry Casley: a salary rise of 18.3 per cent, taking his salary to £258,000, with pension contributions of £27,000.
- Yorkshire Electricity Chief Executive Malcolm Chatwin: a salary rise of 39.2 per cent, taking his salary to £211,354; pension contributions £28,628.
- John Baker, Chief Executive of National Power: a rise of 10.2 per cent, taking his salary to £374,886; pension contributions £62,255.[10]

On 11 August 1994 the newspapers were running front-page stories on the profits made out of consumers by Mr Bryan Weston, the retiring non-executive Chairman of the electricity group Manweb. Manweb provides power to Merseyside, Cheshire and North Wales. *The Daily Telegraph* spelled it out. Mr Weston was Executive Chairman from 1985 to 1992 and saw his earnings shoot up from £79,449 a year in 1989–90 to £156,000 in 1991 and £214,000 in 1992. By 1993 Mr Weston had become the non-executive Chairman and was being paid £75,000 a year for a two-day week. On top of that he received a company car and private health insurance worth a total of £9,000. The *Telegraph*'s City correspondent, Andrew Edgcliffe Johnson, points out that the average non-executive salary in industry is £30,000.

But Mr Weston's bonanza did not stop there. Early in 1994

he exercised his option to buy 141,693 Manweb shares at 307p when they were actually trading at 803p. He thus made a profit of £703,000. He immediately cashed in 27,211 shares, netting £135,000. He still holds 121,878 shares, including 7,390 which he held at the beginning of the year before any options were exercised. If he had decided to sell them in mid-August 1994 they would have been worth £880,000. At the AGM of Manweb held in August 1994 shareholders were bitterly critical, pointing out that the company had made a pre-tax profit of £126m on a £929m turnover and that a disproportionate amount of this was being paid to Manweb directors, who, as at that date, held more than 380,000 shares between them, valued then at £2.77m. Other directors had also traded shares in January 1994, sharing a paper profit of £2.95m between them.

This followed the revelations made the previous week that Eastern Electricity had changed the basis of its bonus payment calculation halfway through 1993 when it became clear that executives would not earn their bonuses due to poor company performance. The result of this was to make John Devaney, Eastern Electricity's Chief Executive, the highest paid director of the twelve privatised regional electricity companies: his bonus of £50,000 took his total pay package to £314,000 a year, up from £255,000 in 1992.

It is possible to add gas and telecommunications as well, but it is the privatisation of water and the truly massive profits accruing to the companies, the telephone number salaries going to their executives and the horrendous rise in water bills which has caused the most disgust.

Let us begin with South West Water, the area where water bills have risen by 150 per cent and where some of the poorest people, including many pensioners, are now paying between an eighth and a tenth of their entire income for a commodity which is essential to life, let alone public health.

This story should really start on 6 July 1988, when a tanker driver arrived at the South West Water Authority's (SWWA) Lowermoor water treatment works in Cornwall. The driver, a relief, had been given a key by the regular driver. Finding the treatment works uninhabited with no trace of a SWWA employee, he tipped his load of aluminium sulphate into the wrong tank, a tank of purified water on its way to the Camelford area. The results were immediate as twenty tons of aluminium sulphate hit the mains supply. Finding their water smelled and was a funny colour, people rang the SWWA to find out what was wrong. They were told there was nothing wrong and it was quite drinkable. Following this reassurance, some 20,000 people did drink it, promptly developing a nasty range of symptoms including sickness, diarrhoea, mouth and nose ulcers, blood in their urine and various aches and pains, while those with arthritis found their condition exacerbated. It was to become known as the Camelford Water Incident.

For some hours SWWA officials refused to believe there was a problem, even after being contacted by local GPs. On 7 July, when 30,000 fish were found dead in the Camel and Allen Rivers, SWWA blamed an equipment failure. On 11 July Douglas Cross, a biologist and water expert living in the area, complained of kidney pains and contacted SWWA. His complaint was rejected although it later transpired that by 8 July SWWA had been aware that aluminium sulphate had got into the wrong tank. At that stage the authority should have alerted everyone to the extent of the disaster. They did nothing. In a report written later, board member Dr John Lawrence said, 'I have observed two reasons why this was not done. No manager took charge in the way implied [i.e. overall control] and there seems to be a culture in which the public are told as little as possible and expected to trust the Authority to look after their interests.' On 19 July, by which time a large number of people were ill, a public meeting was held in Camelford at which Douglas Cross warned people not to drink the water.

SWWA District Manager John Lewis, later sacked for going public, was to make a sworn statement that he had realised as early as 7 a.m. on 7 July that there was possible contamination and knew by 8 July exactly what that contamination was, but he was told to treat the information as strictly confidential and not tell anyone not already aware of the cause. Mr Lewis told his superiors that it was essential a press release was issued but was informed that this could only be done with the approval of the

Chairman and Chief Executive of SWWA, Keith Court. In fact a meeting had been held to discuss whether all that was known should be made public. This idea was vetoed by Mr Court.

On 22 July, sixteen days after the accident, a single advertisement was placed in one issue of the *Western Morning News*. It appeared on the sports page. Headed 'South West Water – Water Supply Quality' and addressed to the 'residents in the Camelford area', it began, 'South West Water wish to assure all their customers in North Cornwall that the water supply is fit to use and drink. The aluminium as delivered to the works was no more acidic than lemon juice and was further diluted many times.' This was the first public admission that there had even been an accident.

There is now ample material available on the Camelford Water Disaster and its aftermath.[11] This includes how, after tremendous pressure for a full investigation, medical tests and a public inquiry, the government sent one elderly scientist to Camelford for half a day to see whether or not people had suffered as a result of drinking the water. She made no tests and reported back to the government that she did not think there were any medical problems: the population was merely suffering from collective hysteria. In the intervening years most of those affected have reluctantly accepted out-of-court settlements, though a handful fight on. SWWA, as it then was, did however successfully claim against the company whose driver made the mistake.

Anger raged throughout Cornwall during that summer of 1988, particularly after the sacking of John Lewis. What people wanted first of all was the head of Chairman and Chief Executive Keith Court on a plate. They demanded he resign; public meetings were held up and down the county to this end. Whenever Mr Court appeared in person he found himself facing baying crowds telling him to go. But he had no intention of resigning, as he continually made clear. For the South West Water Authority was soon to become South West Water plc and Mr Court fully intended to be its new Chairman.

Mr Court is still there. During his last year as Chairman and Chief Executive of SWWA in 1989 he earned £41,000. In 1993 his salary totalled £136,000. The company's Annual Report, published on 26 May 1994, shows pre-tax profits of £93m, up £300,000 on the previous year, dividends up 7.6 per cent, total pay-out to shareholders being £32m, while £54m was ploughed back into the business, including the coastal clean-up. According to these figures each household has contributed £47 to South West Water plc shareholders, averaging 10 per cent of their water bills.[12] Mr Court and his Managing Director, Bill Fraser, told their AGM in May 1994 that the year 1993–94 had been one of sound progress. They believed the increased payments to shareholders were fully justified on the grounds that 'we need to reward our shareholders for their loyalty . . .'

Examples of the financial problems being suffered by consumers in the South West who had seen their bills triple filled the columns of local newspapers. Seventy-nine-year-old Lorna Lowe lives in a one-bedroomed flat on West Hoe in Plymouth, owned by a housing association. She is on income support and her water bill is now £366 a year. Arthur Kenyon, seventy-six, is disabled and lives in Salcombe in South Devon. His water bill is a staggering £677. He asks, as do most South West consumers, why 3 per cent of the population is having to pay for 30 per cent of the coastal clean-up when that 3 per cent live in an area of high unemployment and low wages. He also told the *Western Morning News*, 'I do not see how they can make a profit out of people. I think it is disgusting. It is also disgusting that their managing director should get a huge salary by clobbering people like me.' Eighty-four-year-old Adela Pickard in Okehampton lives alone and has a bill of £450. Lisa and Andy Young live in Sidmouth, South Devon. They are unemployed and have four young children. This year their water bill rose by 25 per cent to £400. They are already £500 in arrears. They now have a water meter to try to help them economise. Economising means flushing the toilet only once a day and taking a bath once a week.[13]

But those who bought shares in South West Water five years ago are laughing. A hundred shares bought in 1989 would have cost £2.40 each, payable in three instalments, £240 in all. Now they are worth £5.15 each, a profit of £275. In the meantime they would have paid out 85.4 pence in dividends per share, with another 17.1p added on in 1994, a total of £1.025 on top of the capital again. So, for an outlay of £240, the investor would now have a profit of over £377, a 157 per cent increase.

Some Chairmen, Chief Executives and directors of water companies have done even better than Keith Court:

- Michael Hoffman, Chief Executive of Thames Water, was given a rise of 14.9 per cent in 1993, bringing his salary up to £247,000.
- Alan Smith, Managing Director of Anglian Water, was given a rise of 3.7 per cent, bringing his salary up to £169,000 with pension contributions of £18,000.
- The highest paid director of Severn Trent Water had a rise of 11.6 per cent, a salary of £218,100 and pension contributions of £83,900.[14]

Water companies also pay out golden goodbyes. When John Bellak, Chairman and Chief Executive of Severn Trent, had his contract terminated in 1994, he received a pay-off of £512,000, while Bob Thian, Chief Executive of North West Water received the even more gargantuan sum of £674,000.

In July 1994 the Labour Party published a handy table showing the increases in water bills, profits and chairmen's salaries:

Water Company	Average Bill			Pre-tax Profit		
	1989	1994	%Increase	1989	1994	%Increase
Anglia	£156	£263	69%	£86m	£132m	54%
Northumbria	£107	£182	65%	£10m	£63m	528%
North West	£111	£182	75%	£75m	£269m	257%
Severn Trent	£106	£179	68%	£139m	£281m	117%
Southern	£125	£201	61%	£60m	£128m	112%
South West	£146	£304	108%	£45m	£93m	105%
Thames	£100	£162	62%	£179m	£242m	35%
Welsh	£147	£256	74%	£40m	£144m	265%
Wessex	£137	£223	62%	£27m	£103m	282%
Yorkshire	£123	£193	57%	£58m	£144m	282%

Water Company	Pre-Selloff	Chairman's Salary Present	% Increase
Anglia	£44,000	£187,000	325%
Northumbria	£40,000	£150,000	275%
North West	£47,000	£338,000	619%
Severn Trent	£51,000	£302,000	492%
Southern	£47,000	£170,000	261%
South West	£41,000	£136,000	231%
Thames	£41,000	£317,000	673%
Welsh	£46,000	£139,000	202%
Wessex	£43,000	£254,000	258%
Yorkshire	£58,000	£156,000	169%

To return to Sir Desmond Pitcher of North West Water and those who think he is worth his salary, according to a second paper published by the Labour Party on 7 August 1994, he actually earns, including bonuses etc, £360,000 a year altogether. It is also pointed out that he is a former Chairman of Littlewoods, which donated £106,450 to the Conservative Party during 1990–92. The paper picks out three other water directors with donating links: John Thompson, a director of Thames Water and Newcastle Breweries, which donated £120,000 in 1992 and 1993; Andrew Simon, director both of Severn Trent and Laporte, the latter having donated £231,200 since 1979; and Ralph Key, a non-executive director of Northumbria Water and also a director of the Cookson Group, which has donated some £60,450 to the party over the years.

The water companies' profits have been described as 'an investor's dream', with operating profits up 20 per cent each year, profit margins up from 28.7 per cent to 35.6 per cent, the industry's total share value up to £13bn from £5.2bn and dividends up by, on average, 58 per cent. As in so many other instances, there have been a few big winners and a lot of small losers.

At the end of July 1994 Ofwat, the water industries' watchdog, decreed that water bills will now be capped to an average of inflation plus 1 per cent. South West Water immediately announced it would be going to the Monopolies and Mergers Commission to see if it could get the decision over-ruled.

Outside the water companies, the Ofwat ruling was received with a good deal of criticism. The *Independent*, in a leading article on 29 July 1994, said, 'But the meek acceptance of the regulator's decision by all the water companies but one should encourage outsiders to smell a rat. Just as the government was too lenient over the past five years, Ofwat's approach on prices over the next ten is little better. If the water industry were properly regulated, prices would fall over the coming decade, not continue to rise.' A point also taken up by the *Guardian,* whose leader commented, 'Of course it is true and necessary that the water industry needs investment in infrastructure to meet environmental health standards. These things cost serious money, which must come in part from increased charges. But the water industry and the regulator are operating in a market rigged by the government to exploit the consumer.

'The regulator's *primary* duty, enshrined in statute, is to ensure that companies can "finance their functions by securing a reasonable rate of return on their capital". His duties to customers – a captive market, remember – are only secondary. The regulator is merely fluting the tune which was written to him in Cabinet. It is hardly surprising that many people may think that the "K factor" used to calculate the new pricing structure refers less to the public interest and more to the knighthoods and thousands of extra pounds on their salaries which the water industry chiefs are now enjoying at their customers' expense.'

Water privatisation was sold on the basis that it would bring in competition. No one has yet explained how this can be brought about; how, for example, a consumer of South West Water might decide to opt for a supply from Thames.

Most things pale beside the megabucks sloshing around in the privatised utilities but, in its own way, the new, market-orientated NHS is doing its best. Two reports published in December 1993[15] show that despite government claims between 1979 and 1991, actual NHS expenditure at the cutting edge was in the region of

22 per cent of total budgets, after adjustment for NHS pay and price inflation, even though the government has claimed it is 50 per cent. But there has been a pay boom for the bosses of the first wave of NHS trusts. Chief Executives' salaries went up by an average of 8.7 per cent in the twelve months to April 1993, while general managers of directly managed units averaged merit rises of 3.6 per cent. Information is hard to find, as many trusts are reluctant to disclose pay rises and restrict access to annual accounts. Some omit details of bonuses and within the trusts there are wide variations. Guy's and Lewisham Trust gave its Chief Executive, Peter Griffiths, a rise of 33 per cent from £103,000 to £137,000 including bonuses, while the Kingston Hospital cut pay by 2.9 per cent. Managers of acute units now earn on average £73,000. The Chief Executives of two trusts, Central Manchester Healthcare and the Liverpool Cardiothoracic Unit, earned over £90,000 each. Public sector workers' rises in the NHS averaged 1.5 per cent.

A total of 651 landowners, including the aristocracy in stately homes and major corporations, have each received £100,000 of taxpayers' money during 1993 not to grow crops. Forty-five farm-owners netted between £250,000 and £500,000 each, while a further seven each received over £500,000 and 2,325 landowners received between £50,000 and £99,999. The payments are part of what is known as 'set-aside' – that is, leaving land uncultivated. Hitherto Ministers have refused to disclose individual payments on the grounds that providing the information would be too costly, but junior Agriculture Minister Michael Jack has now given some information to Labour MP Paddy Tipping. In 1993 farm-owners received £749m under the scheme, a sum set to rise to £924m in 1994. Mr Jack refused to disclose the names of those who have profited, saying only that the biggest single payment was £1.25m.

Finally, though strictly speaking in the competitive market place, the man who must be the envy of all those previously mentioned has to be Martin Sorrell: Martin Sorrell, boss of the advertising group WPP, who presided over the company's near collapse in 1991, will receive a package which could add up to £8m a year. His basic salary, which will be paid through a separate company, will rise from £640,000 to £750,000. He will receive £320,000 in pension contributions. His performance bonus could be worth 100 per cent of his basic pay per annum. He will be able to participate in special share options and he will buy about £2.2m of WPP shares to be put into a special capital programme for him. The company will add 2.5 shares for every one he owns if WPP hits targets. His private health care and personal insurance will be paid. He already has 2.8m options on WPP shares currently at 120p, which would yield a profit of over £1.5m. A company spokesman said, 'We decided we had a chief executive who was as good as we were going to get and wanted to hang on to him. We also wanted him to be highly motivated.'[16]

The question of directors' salaries, free share options and rolling contracts continued to make headlines throughout 1994, particularly with regard to the privatised utilities. The response from the government has always been that these are matters for the companies and their shareholders to decide and are not the affair of government, a view reiterated as late as 22 December 1994 when the Labour Party published a list of Chairmen of utilities who are now millionaires. The Labour Party has said it is committed, when taking office, to regulating the 'gravy train', and taxing the share options and perks awarded to the Chairmen and directors of utilities.

Chapter 8

ROTTEN BOROUGHS –
LAMBETH AND WESTMINSTER

Examples of local government treating its respective town, cities or counties as private fiefdoms are nothing new, nor are they peculiar to Conservative Councils. All political parties and many who label themselves 'independent' have contributed to the findings of a survey published in April 1994 which showed that nearly two-thirds of voters are concerned about corruption in local government.[1]

The survey, *Blowing the Whistle on Fraud and Corruption*, called for Councillors and senior officers to respond to a lack of public confidence in the financial practices of local government. As many as 63 per cent of those polled said they were 'concerned'; 28 per cent were 'very concerned'. Guy Dehn, who is director of the charity Public Concern at Work, told the *Independent* (21.4.94), 'Few Councils have a clear strategy for tackling financial malpractice and fewer still are given any lead by their elected members. For too long the issue has been left to the auditor.'

One-fifth of those surveyed said they had direct experience of fraud and/or corruption in Councils. Almost a quarter had worked for local government or for a contractor. The survey blamed frequent changes in local government organisation over the last ten years for increased opportunities for fraud and corruption. In particular, opportunists were taking advantage of what is described as 'an entrepreneurial culture' in which the pace of 'reforms' had outstripped the development of safeguards against abuses.

Labour's record over the last twenty years has been far from exemplary, from T. Dan Smith on Tyneside in the 1970s, through the manipulations of Derek Hatton and company in Liverpool in the 1980s, to the kind of bizarre activities which went on when Labour controlled Brent. The tabloid press and rent-a-quote Conservative backbenchers had a field day as jobs went to the politically correct, funds were set aside for off-the-twig minority organisations, the whole, more often than not, covered in a fog of incompetence and ineptitude. This provided rich fodder for those who wanted to believe that all Labour Councils, however well run and however much they might struggle to maintain decent services against the odds, were run by Trots and/or the Loony Left. Meanwhile, in the older fiefdoms, especially in the north, 'Alderman Foodbotham', the fictional 'Perpetual Chairman of the Tramways Committee', who used to feature regularly in the *Daily Telegraph*'s 'Peter Simple' column, is still alive and well.

Even nominally 'independent' Councils can wish they had been left out of the spotlight. A recent example is that of North Cornwall District Council which, following a series of media investigations into a whole string of doubtful planning decisions, finally brought on itself the wrath of the Department of the Environment. The DoE, compelled to act, has gone so far as to *order* the Council to demolish a number of properties. At the time of writing, North Cornwall was still refusing to do so, apparently oblivious to the fact that its Planning Department has become a West Country byword for how not to run local government.

There are, however, two Councils – one Labour and one Conservative – which have become synonymous in the public mind with what is wrong with local government.

Lambeth

From the emergence of 'Red Ted' Knight as its leader in 1978, and the subsequent surcharging and forced resignations of Labour Councillors onwards, Lambeth has rarely been out of the news for long: an embarrassment to its party and a soft target for

Conservative attacks. It has continually lumbered from crisis to crisis in what has been well-described as 'a culture of inefficiency'. The borough contains within its boundaries areas which are among the most deprived in the country, with all that that means with regard to lack of resources. It has a huge population of people on the poverty line or below, yet its inefficiency in dealing with housing benefit alone is legendary. Families have actually got to the point of eviction, after months, even years, of trying to sort out their housing benefit with Lambeth, before matters have been resolved. Examples abound of papers lost or mislaid, telephones which are never answered, letters which are unread.

The borough has long been a public relations nightmare. In December 1990, at the same time as it was claiming that lack of cash was at the root of all its problems, it announced that its Mayor was to have a brand new £42,000 'stretch limo'. When this decision, hurried through under its 'Written Urgent Procedure', was criticised, a spokesman replied that it was felt a 'stretch' car would allow access for disabled people.

A month later, in January 1991, Lambeth handed the tabloids another gift by calling for British troops to be pulled out of the Gulf and forbidding staff from flying the union flag, while in the same month it was revealed that British Telecom had cut Council lines thirty times in 1990, on twenty-eight occasions because bills had not been paid. Indeed one housing office was left without phones for a week. Liberal Democrat Councillor Keith Fitchett claimed that only luck had stopped Town Hall electricity supplies from being cut off, not because the money was not there to pay electricity and telephone bills, but because 'they are so incompetent that the bills sit around until BT comes round and disconnects them'.

It was against this background – of continuing financial chaos, an investigation by the national Labour Party and allegations of intimidation by moderate Labour Councillors – that in March 1991 Lambeth's then leader, Joan Twelves, proposed the setting of the highest poll tax charges in the country. The first suggestion was that the poll tax would reach £750 a head, but this was soon reduced to £621, coupled with the loss of a thousand jobs and 141 unfilled posts. Financial analysts put at least some of Lambeth's problems at this time down to the Council's failure, under Ted

Knight, to set a rate back in 1986. Even the setting of a poll tax rate of £621 would mean that the Council would need to raise a budget of £10–£16m, higher than that allowed by the government, and it would, therefore, have led to the Council being 'rate capped' again. Miss Twelves did not assist matters by refusing to pay the poll tax herself while continuing to draw £5,500 a year for attending council meetings.

In January 1993 a Section 5 Report by Lambeth's Chief Executive revealed details of financial mismanagement on a scale described as 'unprecedented in local government history'. Corruption and malpractice were alleged to have cost the Council up to £15m and Councillors were urged to call in the police to investigate. It was claimed, among other things, that £9.5m had been spent unlawfully on highway maintenance and that redundancy payments of £1.8m had been made to Council staff who were then awarded Council contracts; that millions of pounds in housing repair contracts had been paid to sub-contractors without proper tendering and that there was overcharging of up to 138 per cent by the Council's own Direct Labour Organisation (DLO).

In May 1993 came further damning evidence in a report by the District Auditor. It highlighted failures in almost every Council department. The list of irregularities uncovered included £20.2m spent unlawfully on highway maintenance contracts which should have been put out to competitive tender; debts from rents, rates and poll tax arrears amounting to some £173m; the fact that an officer who had been convicted and given a suspended sentence was still working for Lambeth along with three others who had fraudulently claimed benefits totalling several thousand pounds; a tender bid by the DLO was amended by a pre-dated memo which undercut the winning bid by a private firm, but the private firm was then still sub-contracted to do much of the work; DLO officers initiated an illegal £200,000 profit-sharing scheme; Council accounts had been late ever since 1986 with the result that its financial state was still unclear. There was much more in the same vein.

The District Auditor, Paul Claydon, heavily criticised the performance of the Council's financial officers, recommending that Lambeth appoint a new permanent Chief Executive to sort out the mess.

In June 1993 Labour HQ appointed a QC, Elizabeth Appleby, to conduct an inquiry into Lambeth but, up to the time of writing, she has still to report back.

In January 1994 the District Auditor was in the news again, this time for issuing a 'management letter' citing the low benefits take-up which was costing the poorest people in the borough up to £20m and noting that half of all government grant claims were submitted late. It also pointed out that of the sixty-one District Auditor's recommendations for improved financial management, only ten had been implemented on schedule.

Referring to the Council's multi-million pounds benefit administration, the District Auditor concluded that 'resources devoted to the detection and investigation of fraud are totally inadequate'. In February 1994 he again warned about continuing weaknesses in the internal audit section, along with shortage of staff and lack of independence. Figures for 1993–94 showed council tax arrears of £32.2m; a collection rate of only 48 per cent, the worst in the whole country; poll tax arrears dating back to 1990 of £69.3m; and a further debt for old rates and other sundry debtors of £52.6m.

In March 1994, further reports revealed that an additional £9m of spending on sub-contractors had been unlawfully incurred, that around 400 staff had been unnecessarily made redundant at massive cost and that unquantifiable extra costs had been incurred. The District Auditor is currently investigating yet again.

Westminster

'I would go so far as to describe the picture that has emerged as the greatest act of corruption in the history of local government; not financial corruption in the conventional sense, but corruption of the machinery of the authority itself, given over to party political gain in a way – and to an extent – that is absolutely without precedent ... nothing prepared me for such a naked abuse of power, people and resources. I would have said it was unthinkable.'
Andrew Arden, QC.[2]

In January 1994 John Magill, the District Auditor for Westminster, published his interim report into Westminster Council's housing policy. His investigation followed claims made in an edition of the BBC's *Panorama* back in 1989 that Westminster had deliberately fixed its housing policy to ensure a Conservative majority in local Council elections. Presenting his report and its findings, Magill said that in his view 'gerrymandering is a disgraceful and an improper purpose and not a purpose for which a local authority may act'.

The allegations centred around the activities of the Conservative leader of Westminster Council, Dame Shirley Porter. Dame Shirley, a particularly high-profile Council leader and a friend and admirer of Lady Thatcher, had been in trouble previously for selling off Westminster's cemeteries to a developer for a few pence, only to be forced to retrieve them later for several million pounds. When Magill's interim report was published the various newscasts showed copious clips of an event when Dame Shirley, dressed in a bizarre outfit which included a velvet train and a huge feathered hat, met Lady Thatcher, equally garishly turned out and also wearing an extraordinary hat, at some Westminster Council function. You expected them to turn to camera and say, 'No, Cinderella, you can't go to the ball.'

Magill's interim report stated that Dame Shirley and nine other people who had been Council members at the time should be surcharged £21.25m for gerrymandering. The report covered only one aspect of the policy (a second investigation is now underway), the policy of 'designated sales' and 'building stable communities' (BSCs).

The allegation is that Westminster Council used ratepayers' money to pack Tory votes into eight crucial wards to ensure that the Conservatives won the 1990 local elections, which they did indeed win by a landslide. The investigation was taken up once more by the *Panorama* team for a programme scheduled to be transmitted on 25 April 1994. At the last minute it was pulled. Critics said this followed pressure by Conservative Central Office in the run-up to the 1994 local elections; the BBC claimed that a fixed date for the programme had never been set. In the event it did not go out until June, well after the local elections were over. The programme contained new material from Magill's Interim Report, a good deal of hitherto unpublished information culled from literally thousands of Westminster Council documents seized in raids on Council offices (though many had already been shredded) and interviews with those who had been involved in the designated sales and BSC policies.

The core of the whole policy of ensuring a Tory win in the eight crucial wards was masterminded, the report claimed, by Dame Shirley and a small inner circle. The inner circle included her deputy, David Weeks, who has succeeded her as Council leader, and Barry Legg, who was her Chief Whip and is now Conservative MP for Milton Keynes. According to Companies House records, Mr Legg, who denies he was ever involved in discussions regarding the targeting of marginal wards, is a director of the organisation Conservative Way Forward Ltd.[3]

A copy exists of a secret note sent out by Lady Porter, setting out the minimum number of votes needed to win each key ward and the BSC policy which it was hoped would achieve it. Patricia Kirwen, an ex-Conservative Councillor who once stood against Dame Shirley in a leadership contest, told *Panorama* that BSC was 'a very clever public relations name for a very clever policy', developed with the aim of targeting more resources into the eight wards it was necessary to control to win the election. At the time many large old houses were being converted either into offices or into second homes for the very rich. On the face of it, therefore, affordable homes for those with a Westminster connection sounded a praiseworthy objective.

A number of meetings of the inner circle were held at Dame Shirley's country home and also at an Oxford hotel, such gatherings being booked in the name of a non-existent society, the Alvin Toffler Society. Toffler, an American sociologist and author of *Future Shock*, held views much admired by Dame Shirley.

A typical memo from Dame Shirley, printed in the *Observer* on 1 May 1994 and later shown on *Panorama*, states, 'It's extremely important that these papers are dealt with strictly confidentially. Will you please bring this set with you on Saturday. If you're not attending please don't let them out of your sight. In fact when you've read the documents and after we've had our discussion it would be helpful if you swallow them in good spy fashion otherwise they might self-destruct!!'

Another minute of a strategy weekend held on 17–18 September 1988 records the decision being taken that all papers connected with it had to be shredded, the reason given being 'no leaks'.

The fact that Barry Legg now denies knowledge of any such meetings or the designated sales strategy and BSCs prompted Patricia Kirwen to tell *Panorama*, 'I didn't realise he had such a very bad memory. I was present at two or three meetings at which he was also present when the policy and its implementation were being discussed. It's pretty inconceivable he didn't know.' She went on to add that if everything had been proper and above board, then why was it all kept so secret?

All that was needed to ensure the retention of the eight key wards was an overall extra vote of 1,132. To this end a massive programme was initiated. First, blocks of council flats were to be boarded up as they became empty. These were destined for sale to incomers at a reasonable price on the assumption that their gratitude would prompt them to vote Conservative. Next, developers wanting to build yuppy flats were put on a special fast track for planning permission, while hostels and hotels housing Westminster's homeless were to be closed. The homeless, who might be considered to be Labour voters, were to be deported out of the borough and housing officers were specifically told, according to participants in the *Panorama* programme, to be 'mean and nasty' to them.

A particular example of closing a hostel was that of Ambrosden House, which housed homeless young people. Ambrosden was close to the official residence of Cardinal Hume and, when rumours of its closure reached him, he wrote to the Council on 6 July 1988 pleading that the hostel was needed for young people. He told a television news programme that he believed that there was a fundamentally decent side to all individuals, one that is 'generous and decent and I have no doubt I will find it among the Councillors'. As rumours of closure continued to circulate, a reputable housing charity came forward and offered Westminster Council £600,000 to take the responsibility for running the hostel and looking after its residents off its hands. The offer was refused and shortly afterwards the residents of Ambrosden received notification from the Council that the rumours of imminent closure were quite untrue. However, within no time the residents discovered that what had been untrue was the reassurance they had received, not the rumours.

By the end of September 1988 Ambrosden's inhabitants were out on the street and documents show Dame Shirley had earmarked it for closure back in September 1987. Ambrosden had been valued at £2.75m, but it was sold to developers for £630,000 on the grounds that they would provide low-cost flats for sale to those with Westminster connections. Therefore a sum of £2.12m might also be added to the proposed surcharge of Dame Shirley and her colleagues.

Ambrosden was soon converted into flats which were quickly sold off, but not to those with particular Westminster connections. Many went as *pieds-à-terre* for wealthy people with homes in the country; others had no association at all with Westminster. One resident interviewed by *Panorama* confirmed he had had no previous connection with the borough – he had moved in from Fulham and was now working in Docklands. The sale of Ambrosden did, however, achieve its purpose and the Conservatives retained the Victoria ward.

Next, attention turned to Covent Garden and the tenants of Martlett Court. They were informed that the flats were wanted for sale as low-cost housing for first-time buyers and any tenant wishing to leave would be given a grant of £13,000 to enable them to do so. While some people obviously wished to remain where they were, at first even they thought the idea of Building a Stable Community with young first-time buyers seemed a good one and the whole scheme was heavily promoted on that basis. But, as the tenants who still remain now point out, that simply did not happen. As soon as a flat became empty it was bought by a speculator at a knock-down price, done up, and then re-let at sums of between £200 and £300 a week, way over what ordinary working people could afford. The District Auditor considers that the £13,000 grants designed to move people out and so increase votes are likely to have been illegal. He looked at 176 such grants but a further 329 are now under investigation and this might well add a further £4,250,000 to the surcharge. The ward in which Martlett Court stands did, however, remain Conservative.

And so it went on. Throughout the implementation of the policy, Dame Shirley sought the support of the Conservative MP for Westminster North, Sir John Wheeler, now a Northern Ireland Minister, and, indeed, there are film clips of Sir John enthusiastically supporting the BSC policy. Memos exist noting that a 'draft' had gone to 'John Wheeler' to push for grants, of a 'brief going to JW to lobby Ministers' for money to enable the authority to win the local election, money 'for keeping Westminster Tory'.

Sir John proved to be very supportive. On 21 March 1987 he attended a seminar organised by Westminster at the London Business School, most of which was devoted to the policy of designated sales. He now says he has no specific recollection of such a meeting and was 'astonished' when he heard claims made about votes for homes. Patricia Kirwen, who was also there, thought it impossible for him not to have understood, at the very least, the gist of what was taking place. On 3 March 1988 Sir John hosted a meeting in his office at the House of Commons for members of Westminster Council and other MPs where, again, a discussion took place about votes being increased by stepping up the policy of designated sales.

Even street cleaning was targeted in key wards, especially the Zone Improvement Patrols known as 'Zip Teams'. These were introduced officially to provide high-profile cleaning across the whole of Westminster. In reality, they spent most of their time in the key areas as an aid to making their inhabitants 'feel good'. According to John Dyke, Westminster's former Senior Planning Officer, in the end the votes were achieved not only by the use of the Planning Department but by the use of just about every Council service. Everything was geared to BSC which, he said, might as well have stood for 'Building Safer Constituencies'.

'Every council house sale, every special grant and every planning application was matched against the target number of new Tory voters required to register on the electoral roll by October 1989,' claimed *Panorama*, the pace becoming every more furious as four wards appeared to be underperforming. These Dame Shirley referred to as her 'stress wards'.

Throughout the late 1980s, according to John Dyke, Dame Shirley commandeered Council facilities and staff to bring in the Tory vote. Everything was put aside for the top priority, which was targeting. There was, he said, 'a climate of fear from Dame Shirley Porter. Unless officers implemented policies, there was no place for them in the Council.' This was known by everyone, for the climate of fear rippled all the way down. Yet party political funding on the rates is illegal. Asked what the career prospects might be for anyone who had actually spoken out and said it was unlawful, Dyke replied, 'absolutely nil – in Westminster'.

So heavy was the workload by mid-1989 that Dame Shirley brought in a firm of consultants, Victor Hausner Associates, who were employed to assist at a fee of £130,000. A major PR effort was launched to publicise how good everything was in the eight marginal wards. Monitoring became so accurate that the Tories were able to work out which of the key wards were being packed with enough voters and which were not.

But Dame Shirley, it appears, also had another goal. It was essential that Sir John Wheeler, then sitting on a majority of only 3,310, be returned in the next general election. In the autumn of 1989 eyes were cast on the enormous Walterton and Elgin estate in the northern part of his constituency. Dame Shirley had already decided that a squad should be set up to fight Labour, using a campaign of 'dirty tricks'. When tenants on the estate got a whiff of what might be in the air, they decided to use forthcoming new government legislation and bring about a tenants' buy-out of the property, forming themselves into an organisation called WECH (Walterton and Elgin Community Homes) in order to do so. The buy-out attempt was led by a Mr Jonathan Rosenberg.

As the scheme was official government policy, the Council at first appeared to approve it. But such a buy-out would spoil all the plans for filling flats with Tory voters in place of a solid block of Labour votes no effort would ever shift. To buy the flats WECH had to have the approval of the Housing Corporation. Every effort was, therefore, made to persuade the corporation that WECH had neither the finance nor the competence to prove good landlords. As Ken Bartlett, ex-Assistant Chief Executive of the Housing Corporation, told *Panorama*, 'I think they [the Council] felt that their political fortunes would be greatly increased if there was a different demographic make-up.' When that failed, attempts were made to investigate the private life of a member of the corporation.

The next attempt at blocking the sale was the setting up of a rival organisation to WECH, Walterton Residents Against Takeover, with the unfortunate acronym WRAT... Its first meeting was attended by Conservative Westminster Councillors and a small number of Walterton residents. They included Tory supporters Bob and Marie Daniels, who soon backed out as they felt what was proposed was not 'morally right'. A memo noted that Sir John Wheeler should be asked to write to Westminster asking the Council to support WRAT. A letter from Sir John soon arrived at the Council saying that a group of residents had written to him 'begging me to urge upon you the necessity of not allowing this to occur'. A copy of his letter was duly sent to the Housing Corporation. However, as *Panorama* pointed out, there is no proof that Sir John knew of the tricks being played and he has consistently denied any such knowledge. WRAT continually attacked Jonathan Rosenberg personally, but finally went too far when it published a claim that his wife was a supporter of the IRA, a costly blunder for which it had to pay heavily in court.

The Walterton and Elgin estate flats were in very poor condition and, after taking further advice, WECH discovered that they might well be able to charge the Council a considerable sum of money for taking such defective property off its hands. Much depended on what would be in the new legislation on tenants' choice, soon to be introduced by Environment Minister David Trippier. Obviously the advantage lay with those who could discover this information in advance. According to a note, Sir John Wheeler was applied to yet again, this time asking if he would see if he could obtain an advance copy of the guidelines from David Trippier. This would, said Ken Bartlett, have given the Council a distinctly unfair advantage, as both sides were supposed to start with a 'level playing field'. Mr Trippier has since denied leaking a copy to Sir John Wheeler, while Sir John does not remember ever being asked for a copy of the guidelines in the first place and anyway leaks were not the kind of thing he would ever get involved with.

The one piece of good news in this shoddy story is that in the case of the Walterton and Elgin Estate, Dame Shirley lost. WECH won.

Everywhere else the picture was now rosy but for one dark cloud on the horizon: the poll tax. Despite all the millions of pounds and years of effort spent on the charge of gerrymandering, Dame Shirley and her friends were worried that high poll tax bills could sink the ship. Whatever they did and however they played it, it seemed impossible to come up with a figure below the 'psychological barrier' of £200. Westminster's Treasurer, David Hopkins, claims that Barry Legg in particular was determined to get the figure down below £200; the best that could be managed economically was in the region of £270. There was only one way out of the impasse. More government money was needed. The Council, therefore, hired a firm of political lobbyists, GJW, to lobby hard on the question of Westminster's poll tax.

Most remarkably in these straitened times, Westminster's prayers were not only heard but answered. By an amazing stroke of good fortune the Council suddenly received a government windfall of £10.5m. This was made up of £7.3m for 'flood defence', with the useful proviso that Westminster was only actually required to spend £700,000 on it, and a top-up of over £2m which was described as a 'tourism grant'. This had previously been refused. The extra money meant that Westminster could reduce each poll tax bill by £75 and – hey presto! – at £195 Westminster's poll tax was the second lowest in the country.

At the time of writing, neither of these two major causes for concern has been resolved.

It is now well over a year since Labour appointed Elizabeth Appleby QC to investigate the claims of the District Auditor involving not only ineptitude but illegal dealings and unlawful expenditure in Lambeth. In the meantime the residents of Lambeth used their votes in the 1994 local elections to remove a substantial number of Labour Councillors from office.

Dame Shirley Porter, from either Israel or the United States, spent most of the summer of 1994 trying to get John Magill removed from presiding over further hearings on the grounds that his comments on 'gerrymandering' had prejudiced her and her fellow Councillors from getting a fair hearing. She also tried to get the hearings, then set for the autumn, put back yet again on the grounds that she had not had sufficient time to prepare her case.

In October 1994 she finally returned to the UK where she appeared at a fund-raising event at the Conservative Party Conference, alongside Employment Minister Michael Portillo. This caused the *Daily Telegraph* to comment in an editorial that the hearing should go ahead without any further delay and that Lady Porter had had ample opportunity to put her case had she so wished, adding, acidly, that government Ministers should watch the company they kept.

Having failed in her attempt to persuade the relevant authorities to sack Mr Magill, Lady Porter was then faced with the unprecedented spectacle of Mr Magill sitting in public at Marylebone Town Hall, deciding whether or not to sack himself: not surprisingly he declined. Her further strenuous efforts to have the hearings set back also came to nothing, it being pointed out that she had had five and a half years to make her case, had consistently refused to return to the UK to make it (and indeed had suggested that Magill and his team fly out to Israel at public expense to hear her explanation there) and that there was no possible excuse for any further delay. Neither Ted Knight of Lambeth nor Derek Hatton of Liverpool had been allowed anything like so much time to explain themselves before action was taken against them.

On 19 October 1994 the hearings finally opened. At one time it had seemed that Lady Porter would not appear in person, leaving her defence to her lawyers, but she did finally turn up, to be met by jeering crowds – proving, she told TV reporters waiting outside, that she had no hope of a fair hearing, having been tried and condemned by the media.

Andrew Arden, representing the protesting ratepayers, has sifted through some 6,000 of the 10,000 pages of documents collected by the District Auditor, a number of which, of an extremely damaging nature, were shown on BBC's *Newsnight* on 14 October. Before the hearings Arden said that there were moral dimensions emerging from the investigations into what had gone on in Westminster.

'They are about values and conduct. They are about what is meant by local government professionalism. They are about what goes on behind closed doors, and about how the money raised by local taxation is spent. They are about authority, and its use or abuse – members over officers, officers over one another. They are about withholding information from minority members. They are about deceit.' What was at stake was the corruption of the whole machinery of local government.

Chapter 9

HONOURABLE MEMBERS

'Some MPs have their noses so far in the trough you can see the soles of their feet.'
Paul Flynn, Labour MP for Newport West.

'When they stand in the village hall wearing a rosette and saying "Vote for me", they don't say "Send me to Parliament and as soon as I get there, I'll get my snout in the trough." '
Dennis Skinner, Labour MP for Bolsover.

'People out there already think we all have our xxxxx in our secretaries and our hands in the till.'
Unnamed senior politician quoted by Andrew Rawnsley in the *Observer*.

Current opinion polls show that politicans have never been held in so little public esteem. While two of the MPs quoted above are Labour members, anxiety is not confined to the Opposition benches. Hugo Young writing in the *Guardian* just before the 1994 parliamentary summer recess under the heading 'A Lingering Stink in the Tale of the Tory Party Piggy-Bank' noted, 'Sleaze is the sleeping issue. It continues to petrify many Ministers in this government . . . they worry a lot in private about the overarching possibility that they are regarded as a government of crooks that Asil Nadir helped to power.'
Public cynicism is due, in part, to the well-publicised cases of

government Ministers and Conservative MPs at all levels who have continually banged on about public morality, Victorian values and so on, only to be revealed as tacky adulterers and/or the fathers of children born to those castigated single mothers. Few people expect politicians to live lives of blameless sexual rectitude, but blatant hypocrisy sticks in the gullet.

However, while affairs with actresses or call girls and even bastard children briefly make the headlines and are soon forgotten, the overall unease has far more to do with a general suspicion that representing the voters of the constituency for which he or she has been elected comes pretty low on the priority list of those we now send to Parliament.

In January 1994 MPs voted themselves a pay increase of 2.7 per cent, bringing the salary of an ordinary backbencher up to £31,687.[1] Inflation, at that time, was running at less than 2 per cent. It was a little higher when, in August 1994, it was announced that MPs' salaries were to rise by nearly 5 per cent (twice the rate of inflation) from January 1995, further increasing salaries to £33,169. This is made up of a pay rise of 2.7 per cent, plus the reinstatement of the old link between MPs' pay and that of Grade 6 civil servants. Allowances will rise accordingly.

For, on top of their salaries, MPs have a whole range of perks. Car allowance is based on mileage and size of car engine. For cars with engines under 1,300cc the allowance is 28.8 pence a mile for the first 20,000 miles and 15.1 pence after that. A car with an engine of more than 2,300cc rates a luxurious 68.2 pence a mile for the first 20,000 miles and 34.1 pence thereafter. In addition MPs get free travel by rail, sea or air between the triangle of home, constituency and Parliament and can claim many other travel expenses on parliamentary business. Their wives and children under the age of eighteen get the same free travel arrangements between constituency and London for up to fifteen trips a year. MPs get free stationery, inland telephone calls and postal services from Parliament. They get an expense allowance to cover secretarial and research assistance of £40,380 at the time of writing. They can also claim for extra assistance if their secretary or researcher is temporarily absent, up to a maximum period of twenty-six weeks.

MPs with inner London constituencies have a London supplement of £1,222 added to their income, while those with constituencies outside can claim up to £11,000 a year for additional expenses for overnight stays on parliamentary business. An average backbencher with a constituency in the provinces receives, therefore, some £82,000 a year of taxpayers' money. Pension arrangements are good and MPs contribute only 6 per cent towards them. In July 1994 ex-Defence Minister Alan Clark, one of the wealthiest men in Parliament, claimed in his *Mail on Sunday* column that most MPs' emoluments came close to £100,000 with everything taken into consideration. He went on to say that he did not know what half the MPs needed offices for and that any MP who felt like it could 'give his computer to his wife or, if she's giving trouble, his girlfriend'. The only time he had his 'second home allowance' for his London flat challenged was 'when I tried to buy replacement glasses from Asprey rather than IKEA'.

Holidays are generous. Between December 1993 and October 1994 MPs had over a fortnight during the Christmas break, a fortnight at Easter, a further fortnight in May for reasons which are not quite clear, and the summer recess, commencing in mid-July and lasting until after the Party Conference season, well into October; and this at a time when we are continually informed there is a terrible shortage of time for getting Bills through Parliament and many Private Members' Bills, even those with all-party support, fall by the wayside. Looking abroad, the US Congress was still in session at the end of August and the French deputies took only four weeks.

However, as has frequently been pointed out, in reality there are two kinds of MP: those who depend entirely on their Parliamentary earnings and those who supplement these with directorships, adviserships, consultancies and so on. On average a consultancy brings in about £10,000 a year, a directorship £15,000, although both figures fluctuate. Some consultancies can go up to £60,000 and, as in the privatised utilities and big business, most directorships are combined with potentially lucrative shareholdings and share options. MPs can earn further commission for introducing their 'clients' to merchant bankers, stockbrokers, investment firms and lobbying companies.

Another way of adding to earnings is, of course, to become some kind of a Minister. It is surprising, in view of the way Ministers and their departments are shedding responsibilities to Quangos and privatised agencies, to discover that the number of Ministers on the government payroll has increased from a mere fifty-nine in 1905, when Britain ruled a huge empire, to the present 108. Indeed there is a plethora of junior ministerial posts in almost every department, some holders of such offices only coming to public notice when their more senior colleagues are on holiday and they are left to represent their departments. Yet since 1979 the civil service payroll has been almost halved and the administrative role of government drastically reduced.

It was the Liberal government of 1905 which had fifty-nine Ministers; by 1915 the Asquith administration had sixty-three. After the Lloyd George government fell in 1922, the incoming Conservatives appointed seventy-one. By 1951, under Labour, there were 105, but this had been reduced by the time the Conservatives left office in 1974 to eighty-nine. Now the payroll has risen again. On top of this are the unpaid Parliamentary Private Secretaries (PPSs) who are backbench MPs. Apart from anything else this large number of office-holders, in the present instance about a third of all Conservatives in Parliament, ensures what is known as 'the payroll vote': those with ambition can be relied on to vote the right way and not make any trouble.[2]

On a smaller scale there is the wining and dining. In July 1994 Labour MP Paul Flynn elicited the information that the two largest dining rooms at the House of Commons, those next to the Thames, had been booked 1,399 times in twelve months by Conservative MPs and 167 times by Labour. He and Labour MP Alan Williams claimed that some Conservative members apparently 'touted' for business at such events. In the same week Sir David Steel of the Liberal Democrats revealed that he had refused a five-figure offer to book such a dining room and host events there for corporate clients. An investigation instigated by *The Sunday Times* (17.7.94) on learning of this revealed that some MPs regard the booking of the private dining rooms for money as just part of their consultancy work. Sir Malcolm Thornton, Conservative MP for Crosby, hosted receptions for Singapore Airlines at the Commons and received payment as part of an overall 'advisory' retainer with Keene Public Relations Consultants. Sir Jerry Wiggin, Tory MP for Weston-super-Mare, hosts a dinner every other year on the eve of the Boat Show for the British Marine Industries Federation, for which he is paid an undisclosed fee for acting as their adviser. He told the paper, 'I don't see why a company should be deprived if they have a friendly MP to host a party for them.' An unnamed senior Tory is quoted as receiving £5,000 a year as a consultant whose main function is simply to hire rooms for lunches and dinners and persuade junior Ministers to attend. All have declared their interests in the various firms in the Register of Members' Interests. The head of one firm which pays MPs to book Commons' dining rooms told *The Sunday Times,* 'We send out the invitations, but we are not allowed to book rooms at the Commons. The MP books the room and acts as host. It is still one of the cheapest forms of entertainment we can do. We can get meals at the Commons for £24 a head. Compare that to the Savoy Grill!'

So what kind of consultancies and directorships do MPs take up to supplement their incomes? All MPs are supposed to register their outside interests with the Register of Members' Interests. This practice dates back over twenty years to the scandal surrounding the property developer John Poulson, but in general an MP only hits the headlines for failing to declare an interest when some particular aspect of it achieves notoriety. Registration should include any paid company directorships or consultancies; professional occupations, trades and vocations; the names of clients of companies with whom the MP is retained as a consultant or director which arise out of his/her being an MP; financial sponsorship including gifts of over £125; overseas visits funded by private industries; payments from foreign governments, agencies or individuals; ownership of land and property; companies in which the MP or a spouse has shareholdings over 1 per cent; and the names of specific Lloyds syndicates of which an MP has a membership.

As Paul Halloran and Mark Hollingsworth point out in their excellent guide to MPs' interests, *A Bit on the Side*,[3] some things are noticeably missing. These include the actual amount paid to an MP for what he undertakes to do; shareholdings of less than one per cent; value and size of declared shareholdings; nature of services provided by an MP for a client; clients of public relations and private consultancy companies set up by MPs themselves. Worst of all, it must also be pointed out that registering such interests is voluntary, not statutory, and the Register itself is based only on guidelines. MPs are only *obliged* to declare a particular interest when making a speech in debate or in committee proceedings. They do not have to declare a particular interest when asking oral questions, submitting written questions, making 'brief' interventions during a debate or sponsoring Commons' motions. This anomaly was at the heart of what became known as the 'Cash for Questions' scandal which will be dealt with later.

Halloran and Hollingsworth claim that particularly during the Thatcher years, many MPs spent at least as much time looking after their own private financial interests as they did on remembering their constituencies, quoting Edwina Currie in the April 1991 edition of *New Woman* magazine: 'There was a colleague who told the Whips he was in his constituency and he told his constituency that he was in London. In fact, he was in the Channel Islands, running a business. Another colleague lives in California and only comes to Westminster about six times a year.'

It would obviously be impossible to list all the MPs and the interests they have either noted in the Register or those which have been discovered through diligent searches at Companies House. A few examples must suffice. Sir Michael Grylls, Conservative MP for Surrey South West, is a busy man. He is a member of the Commons Select Committee on Trade and Industry and is often referred to by the media when they are looking for a spokesperson. He is a director of Le Carbone Lorraine (GB) Ltd, Armstrong Consulting Services Ltd, Columbus Holdings Ltd, Electrophoretics plc. He is a consultant to the Association of Authorised Public Accountants, adviser to the Unitary Tax Campaign, consultant to Sanofi Winthrop Ltd, Digital Equipment Ltd, Charter Consolidated plc and the National Federation of Post Offices and BT Pensioners. He names as clients the powerful lobby firm Ian Greer Associates. In 1990 a Select Committee inquiry found that Sir Michael had received three 'thank-you' payments for introducing new clients to Ian Greer Associates. These were not properly declared at the time and his association with the lobby organisation was only registered in October 1989, some time after he had received the payments.[4]

Another prominent Conservative spokesman is Sir Marcus Fox, Chairman of the powerful backbench 1922 Committee. Directorships are Westminster Communications, a lobby company; contract cleaners Care Services Group; McCarthy and Stone plc; the Hartley Investment Trust; Bristol Port Co; Illingworth Morris Ltd, and the Yorkshire Food Group. He is a consultant to 3M (UK), Shepherd Construction and electrical engineers Gratte Brothers; clients are Westminster Communications, British Gas, the Builders Merchant Federation and Standard Life. According to Companies House, he is also a director of First Corporate Shipping Ltd and the John McCarthy Foundation.

Sir Marcus's predecessor as Chairman of the 1922 Committee, Sir Cranley Onslow, Conservative MP for Woking, lists directorships in Redifon Holdings Ltd (of which he is also the Chairman) and Elmdale Investments Ltd; and consultancies with the Argyll Group plc, Bristow Helicopters, LEK Partnership and Generic Holdings Corporation. Searches in Companies House also revealed he was a director of the ACA Trustee Company Ltd and the Nautical Museum Trust.

The Rt Hon. David Mellor MP, who resigned as Secretary of State for National Heritage after his well-publicised affair with an actress, as well as cropping up as a *Guardian* columnist and BBC Radio personality and presenter, is a director of Abela Holdings UK Ltd and of three arts charities (unpaid). He is a consultant to the Middle East Broadcasting Centre, Middle East Economic Digest, GL Holdings (Bermuda), RACAL Tacticom Ltd, Millwall Holdings plc, Crosby Associates UK, Investcorp, Shandwick Consultants, and Ernst and Young. He works as a public relations consultant for Shandwick. His other consultancy work is on business development not related to his work as an MP. Halloran and Hollingsworth point out that Mr Mellor has acquired an impressive list of PR clients. As well as being Heritage Secretary, he has also been Chief Secretary to the Treasury, served at the Home Office twice and as junior

Minister in the Departments of Energy and Health and in the Foreign Office.

The Rt Hon. Michael Jopling, Conservative MP for Westmoreland and Lonsdale, sits on the Foreign Affairs Select Committee. He is a director of Blagden Industries plc and is a consultant to Hill and Knowlton (UK) Ltd. He lists his 'trade' as farmer and he is a member of Lloyds. He is a shareholder in Ryelands Properties Ltd and his clients include the Police Superintendents Association, the Royal Armouries, Chiquita Brands International, Vernons Organisation, Nuclear Electric, Vaux plc, Railtrack, American Express, European Recovery and Recycling Association, Union Bank of Switzerland and Games for Good Causes plc.

Michael Mates, Conservative MP for East Hampshire, was another resignation candidate, in his case over his advocacy on behalf of Asil Nadir. In 1986 he became Chairman of the Commons Select Committee on Defence while in the same year also becoming a consultant to Link Miles Ltd, a major defence contractor. In 1990 he became a consultant to a PR company, SGL Ltd, which acts for defence companies. A Commons inquiry found Mr Mates was 'in error' for not declaring these interests properly during Defence Select Committee hearings. It was in 1993, by which time he was Northern Ireland Security Minister, that his championship of Asil Nadir proved an embarrassment to the government, not least because of his sending the wanted man a watch engraved with the words 'Don't let the buggers get you down'.

Jonathan Aitken, Conservative MP for Thanet South and a winner in the 1994 summer reshuffle, became Minister for Defence Procurement in 1992. He had had long-standing business links with Saudi Arabia and was a director of Al-Bilhad UK Ltd, which received payments from contracts with the Saudi Arabian royal family and government agencies. He was also Deputy Chairman of Aitken Hume, a financial services group which was used to channel £1.2m of Saudi royal funds to buy a stake in TV-AM plc.

Perhaps it should also be mentioned here that forty-four Conservative MPs, including four Cabinet Ministers, are members of Lloyds syndicates and were allowed to vote on the 1992 Finance

Bill, even though they were faced with a direct conflict of interest on key clauses.

Whenever the Labour Party draws attention to the lists of directorships and consultancies attached to the names of Conservative MPs, the riposte is that many Labour members are sponsored by trade unions and thus influenced by them. Indeed many are, the single largest group being sponsored by the Transport and General Workers' Union. These include ex-party leader Neil Kinnock (at the time of writing about to become an EEC Commissioner) and the new Labour leader, Tony Blair. Any remuneration paid to Mr Kinnock is listed as going directly to constituency party funds, while Mr Blair has received no personal payments at all, but lists small sums from trade unions and the Rowntree Trust to pay for research. Most union financial sponsorship appears to consist of contributions towards election expenses and/or research and annual grants to constituency parties.

For years the name of Sir Eldon Griffiths, who was Conservative MP for Bury St Edmonds, was synonymous with that of the Police Federation. Hedging its bets, the federation now sponsors two MPs: Michael O'Brien, Labour MP for Warwickshire North and now a non-practising solicitor in criminal law, and Michael Shersby, Conservative MP for Uxbridge. Mr O'Brien receives financial assistance to employ a researcher. Mr Shersby does not list whether or not he is paid personally, but his private secretary receives a fee from the federation. More controversial is Labour's Dr Jack Cunningham. Throughout the time he acted as Labour's Shadow Environment Secretary (1983–89), he was a paid policy adviser to Albright and Wilson (UK) Ltd, and Leather Chemicals. Dr Cunningham's constituency of Copeland also houses British Nuclear Fuel's notorious Sellafield plant, which can always count on him to support them. Dr Cunningham now also lists adviser to Hays Chemicals and Centurion Press Ltd. He is sponsored by the General and Municipal Workers' Union as both a candidate and a member, with direct benefit to him.

Among Liberal Democrats with consultancies is Alan Beith, MP for Berwick-on-Tweed, who lists Magellan Medical Communications Ltd, the Bourne Leisure Group Ltd, advisership to the

Association of University Teachers and clients of Magellan Medical Communications, the Pharmaceutical Contraceptive Group, Schering Healthcare, Wyeth Laboratories, Organon, Cilag and Parke-Davis. On the whole, though, as is the case with the majority of Labour MPs, Liberal Democrats' consultancies and sponsorship run to the kind of activities listed by Simon Hughes, Liberal Democrat MP for Southward and Bermondsey: a £1 share in the Director of Cambridge University Mission; a £1 share in the Rose Theatre Trust Ltd and a further £1 share in the Thames Heritage Parade Ltd!

On 4 September 1994 the *Observer* produced its own trawl of MPs' extra earnings. Senior Tory backbencher Sir Peter Emery was paid commissions totalling £500,000 over three years for property deals involving a company of which he was Chairman, in addition to the £24,000–£29,000 he earned as Chairman of the Winglaw Group. He described the payments as 'nothing extraordinary'. Junior Ministers Gerry Malone and Ian Taylor received income from consultancies and directorships worth more than twice their salaries as MPs. MP David Evans' private company received fees likely to reach £300,000 in the 1994 financial year. Labour, which gives the impression that few, if any, of its MPs make money outside the House of Commons, has not drawn attention to Geoffrey Robinson, who earned £100,000 in 1993 from the engineering group Trans Tec, of which he is Chairman, along with payments from two other companies. The going rate for an MP to sit on a board is between £5,000 and £15,000.

Just how much time all this leaves for Parliament is open to question. As the late David Penhaligon, Liberal MP for Truro, put it succinctly, 'I've always said you could divide the House into three categories for how hard they work. About a third work very hard, really hard, a fifteen-hour day would be the norm and they're workaholics really, but the other 200 probably do a reasonable day's work, and there's 200 which, if you can discover anything they do, let me know.'

As has already been said, it is not possible to discover just how much remuneration any MP receives for each consultancy, advisership or directorship. This is described as a 'right to privacy', a right which is hotly defended. In a Commons debate on the subject in 1985, Liberal Democrat leader Paddy Ashdown said, 'When a person joins this House he is involved in the business of public affairs and must therefore relinquish some of that privacy . . . Privacy often leads to secrecy, and secrecy is the blanket behind which corruption can take place. I therefore believe that there is a need to declare all sources of cash over and above parliamentary salaries. There is only one loyalty that Members of this House have and that is loyalty that is derived from the vote cast in the ballot box.'

Cash for Questions

So to the matter which has brought it all to a head: the Cash for Questions scandal. The rumour that some MPs were being paid to ask parliamentary questions on behalf of outside interests is not new and *The Sunday Times*, which was responsible for bringing it to the public notice, did not just pluck the notion out of the air. To discover whether or not it was true, therefore, a journalist, in the guise of a businessman, contacted a number of MPs and asked if they would be prepared to ask a parliamentary question for him for a fee of £1,000. Ten Conservative and ten Labour MPs were asked. The result was that four Conservatives were willing to ask questions. Bill Walker, MP for North Tayside, asked for the money to be sent to charity and Sir John Gorst, MP for Hendon North, said he would do it for nothing, while suggesting he might be happy to discuss a future arrangement.

Two MPs, David Tredinnick, MP for Bosworth, and Grahame Riddick, MP for Colne Valley, both Parliamentary Private Secretaries, agreed to do so with little demur. Tredinnick, aged forty-four, is an Old Etonian and former Guards officer, once described by the *Daily Telegraph* as having a staccato delivery which suggests he is using most of his words for the first time. As his name suggests, he is of Cornish origin and comes from generations of inherited wealth from tin mining. Riddick, aged thirty-eight, was the darling of the right-wing tabloid press, always ready with a quote. His grandfather was an MP, his father a mill-owner and he went to public school. Before arriving in Parliament he had been a sales manager for Coca-Cola. Treddinick was PPS to Sir Wyn Roberts at the Welsh Office, Riddick to John MacGregor, then Transport Secretary.

A few days before the story broke Riddick was on his feet during Scottish Question Time asking if there were plans to abolish the Labour-run Monklands Council, the constituency of the late John Smith. 'Do not the revelations of corruption, nepotism and dubious job practices in Monklands during the recent by-election vindicate Conservative members who have pointed to the corruption in that Council? How many other Labour Councils are getting up to similar shenanigans?' Yet only the previous afternoon, Mr Riddick had entertained an unknown 'businessman' to tea on the terrace of the House of Commons. The businessman had approached Riddick with a proposition. He was thinking of buying a firm called Githins Business Resources and wanted to know what government contracts it had. Riddick asked off-handedly what it was worth. The businessman replied, '£1,000.' 'That's fine,' said Riddick. Later the reporter telephoned Riddick and taped the conversation. Riddick confirmed he was happy to go ahead. He would tell 'the members' interests people' that it was a July 1994 consultancy project. There followed a dicussion of when the question could be asked, after which the journalist, for it was he, asked, 'What do you want me to do about paying the £1,000? Would you like me to put the cheque in with the résumé or would you rather do it after the question has been raised?' Riddick replied, 'I don't really mind. Why don't you just send it to me? Do you want my home address?' He then gave it. A further conversation took place the following day.

Two days after the conversation on the terrace with Riddick, Tredinnick entertained the same 'businessman' in the same place. This time the inquirer wanted to know how many times a drug called Sithgin had been prescribed on the NHS, as he wanted to invest in the company. Tredinnick said he thought the discussion was to be about a consultancy, to which the reporter replied that he did not know if Tredinnick did that kind of work. 'It's hardly work,' replied Tredinnick. 'But I mean I will pay for it,' said the reporter. Tredinnick began to say he wasn't sure whether . . . when the reporter added, 'It's worth about £1,000 to me.' 'OK,' said Tredinnick. 'Well, I'm just going to check with the upstairs office to see what they think of it [i.e. the question, not the fee]. I don't see any reason why I shouldn't proceed.' Pressed to ask the question quickly, Tredinnick agreed. The reporter asked if he would like to be paid there and then as he had a cheque already made out. Tredinnick replied that was very kind but he could send the cheque to him in the post. The address to which the cheque should be sent was then double-checked.

The Sunday Times marvelled at Tredinnick taking the bait, pointing out that £1,000 is a drop in the ocean to a man who reputedly lost around £1.5m as a Lloyds name. He is a member of some nineteen syndicates. Riddick is also a Lloyds loser.

When the news broke both MPs were immediately suspended from their posts as PPSs. Both tried to bluster it out, protesting their innocence. Tredinnick, who had specified that the sum should go to his private address, said he had been intending it should go to charity. Riddick subsequently returned the cheque. Senior party members rushed to defend the two, casting the media in the role of the villain of the piece, pointing out that the men had, strictly speaking, done nothing legally wrong. Riddick told the *Guardian*, 'What I have found staggering is that a journalist from *The Sunday Times*, presumably with the connivance of the editor, should tell me a tissue of lies simply to manufacture a story when neither illegality nor impropriety was being investigated.' Tredinnick, whose conversations with the reporter are on tape, told BBC Radio, 'I acted in good faith to help him. I did not expect to receive a cheque. I refused to accept a cheque and in any case if I had agreed to do so, providing I had registered that interest, I would not have been in any way contravening regulations.'

Predictably attitudes divided along party lines, Conservative MPs blaming the media in general and *The Sunday Times*, which they had always seen as one of their own, in particular, while Labour had a field day with the kind of quotes that headed this chapter. There were, however, a number of senior Conservatives who were far from happy at the attitude taken by their more vociferous colleagues.

On 14 July the House debated the issue when at least as much, if not more, time was given to the issue of supposed 'entrapment'. Tredinnick remained silent throughout the debate. Riddick, however, apologised, while at the same time attacking the paper which had caught him out. 'I very much regret what I hope the House will accept was a lack of judgement on my part,' he said. 'I was unwise to have even considered what he asked me to do. I accept I made an error of judgement in agreeing to table a question and initially agreeing a fee.' The furious attack on the media was led by Sir John Gorst who, it might be remembered, had offered to ask a question for nothing but with the possibility of discussing matters further. Sir John, whose PR clients have included Alfred Marks, the British Amusement Caterers' Association, Kodak, Capital Radio, Grunwicks, the Contract Cleaning and Maintenance Association and others, raged about 'these so-called guardians of the public interest who are arrogating ... the right to break the law, the right to offer felonious bribes, the right to invade the precincts and privileges of parliaments. Such contemptible arrogance has not been seen since the days of the robber barons.' Those who sought to persuade an MP to accept bribes were guilty of contempt. Secret tape-recordings of conversations should be banned at Westminster and *The Sunday Times* barred from the building. 'Who are these members of the Fourth Estate anyway?'

Rupert Allason MP, who writes books on the secret service under the pseudonym Nigel West, pontificated that 'investigative journalism is not a licence to invade privacy', a response which might well lead one to ask why an elected representative who takes money to put down a question in Parliament, supposedly part of an open democratic process, should require privacy?

On the other hand, veteran Labour MP Tony Benn argued that all MPs should have to publish all their outside interests from the time they put in their nomination papers before an election. As to consultancies, 'We are elected to be consultants to the British people. Why else do we come here? There are two views of privilege. One view is that it is to prevent MPs being criticised outside. I believe privilege is there to protect the electors so that Parliament, which they have elected, can perform its functions.'

In the event MPs agreed without a division that a committee of senior MPs would be set up to consider the allegations against the MPs and also those of entrapment, although it would be unlikely to report before the end of the year.

On 30 July *The Sunday Times* was cleared by the Press Complaints Commission of using unethical entrapment techniques in its investigation. The commission concluded that the subterfuge used was justified because it was the only investigative tool available and the subject raised serious issues of public interest which it was right to pursue.

The Sunday Times itself, commenting on the whole affair, said there had been worse weeks for the House of Commons, 'but not many', not least because one Tory MP after another who spoke in the debate had chosen to add to the embarrassment of their party. 'Rarely can such a group of self-interested, self-deluded and self-important backbenchers have shown such a disregard for the low esteem in which they are held by most people in this country.' Their contribution to the debate was 'wretched, full of tetchiness, pettiness and feeble attempts to deflect attention on to *The Sunday Times* for revealing two dishonourable members. Far from allaying the fears that MPs are not disinterested representatives of the electorate, they merely succeeded in reinforcing the suspicion that many are interested mainly in lining their own pockets.'

The Register of Members' Interests, the newspaper continued, has become a device which certain MPs can use to appear to behave responsibly while using their position to make easy money. 'They have merely to list their interests in the Register, a Register which is generally uninformative, largely voluntary and makes no mention of whether an MP is being paid £50 or £50,000 for a consultancy. This is in stark contrast to local government where it is a criminal offence for Council members to hide a financial interest. . . . The House of Commons,' it concluded, 'has to be a respected legislature, not a Levantine bazaar. Its Arthur Daley tendency has to be rooted out.'

On 20 July 1994, after much criticism, the names of those who would sit in judgement were announced. There was immediate criticism from Opposition MPs because a number of the Conservative appointees themselves held outside consultancies and directorships. They included Sir Marcus Fox (see interests above); Sir Cranley Onslow (likewise); Sir Peter Hordern (three director-ships and a consultancy) and Sir Giles Shaw (ex-Minister, with directorships in Yorkshire Water, British Steel and Broadcasters Audience Research, and a consultancy with the Philip Harris Group). On 19 October 1994, two days after Parliament returned from its long summer holiday, it was confirmed that all hearings would be in camera, as a result of which Labour and Liberal Democrat MPs withdrew from the committee.

That evening Labour MP Stuart Bell went to the despatch box of the House of Commons to raise a matter which was to fill the front page of the following day's *Guardian*: the allegation, backed up by documentary evidence, that two junior Ministers, Neil Hamilton and Tim Smith, had accepted cash for questions when they had been backbenchers. Hamilton's brief, at Trade and Industry, was 'business probity and deregulation'; Smith was at the Northern Ireland Office. Smith is recorded in *A Bit on the Side* as putting down fifty-eight parliamentary questions to government departments in February 1988, asking for detailed information on consultancy contracts.

The *Guardian* report claimed that a Westminster lobbying com-pany, Ian Greer Associates, was paid tens of thousands of pounds to give to the two MPs for asking questions at £2,000 a time on behalf of Harrods during the battle for control of the store between the Al-Fayeds and Lonrho. Ian Greer has consistently denied these allegations and claims he has never acted improperly.

At the end of October, faced with a torrent of allegations of sleaze, John Major announced the setting up of a Special Committe under the Chairmanship of Lord Nolan. At first its inquiry was to be limited to looking into the conduct and interests of Members of Parliament, but its remit has now been substantially widened. It will also look into the appointment and conduct of Quango members and the ethics and conduct of civil servants. In a preliminary paper published on 6 December 1994, Lord Nolan gave details of the committee's brief at the hearings, which would begin in the middle of January 1995 and continue for about six weeks. Already some thousand submissions have been received from members of the public. The committee will be looking at general rules, not individual allegations of corruption, and will consider the possibility of putting forward a set of principles to back up the present system of judicial supervision, the remit of the Select Committees, independent monitoring of local government, codes of ethics in business and an administrative code for civil servants and Ministers. It will also set out a range of options for controlling the outside interests of MPs and ask whether a valid distinction can be drawn between an MP's trade or profession and a paid consultancy on behalf of an interest group, and whether MPs whose money from outside interests exceeds a certain amount should be paid less from public funds.

Its remit will not, however, cover the issue of cash for questions. At the time of writing a date for the deliberations of the Committee of Privileges has yet to be set. However, the Labour and Liberal Democrat members have now decided, after all, that they will sit on it.

Chapter 10

'DO AS I SAY, NOT AS I DO'

When members of the public are stopped by reporters and asked their views on the current political climate in general and high-profile politicans in particular, the most common adjective used is 'hypocritical'. Chancellors or ex-Chancellors who sermonise on the theme of public thrift yet use public money to fund their own court cases. MPs who make a fast buck buying and selling discounted Council housing, fathers of illegitimate children who castigate single mothers and others of a similar ilk have all played their part in bringing about that climate, as the following examples show.

'Astonishingly Good Value. . . .'

It was way back in 1991 that the then Chancellor, Norman Lamont, ran into a little difficulty with the tenant to whom he had let the basement of his London house when he moved into his rent-free accommodation at 11 Downing Street.

The *News of the World* put the problem succinctly in its headline of 13 April 1991: 'Chancellor's Flat is a Vice Den!' It was obvious that the Chancellor had to rid himself of his embarrassing tenant, Sara Dale, who described herself as a 'sex therapist', not least because on the day the story broke he had been attending a meeting of the G7 international Finance Ministers. This much is understandable. As Sir Peter Middleton, former Treasury

Permanent Secretary was to point out later when called to explain what happened next, the media were 'trying to make a connection between her and the Chancellor'. Like all government departments, the Treasury is well stocked with legal experts and it might be imagined that Mr Lamont would have turned to them to sort out his predicament, a simple task which any jobbing solicitor could have accomplished. Not so.

In January 1993 it emerged that the Chancellor had gone outside Whitehall and employed one of the country's most expensive lawyers, Peter Carter Ruck, and that the bill for evicting the lady had run to a mind-bending £23,000, of which we, the taxpayers, had contributed £4,000 plus £700 VAT. The balance had very kindly been paid for the Chancellor of the Exchequer by an anonymous Conservative benefactor. Faced with an electorate reeling from proposed tax increases and endlessly exhorted to tighten their belts, the House of Commons Public Accounts Committee called three senior civil servants before it to justify paying out £4,700 of taxpayers' money for a job that could have been done in-house at a fraction of the final bill.

Sir Peter described Mr Carter Ruck's work – at £260 per hour – as 'astonishingly good value. I think it was very cheap.'[1] In this he was backed up by no less a person than the head of the Civil Service itself, Sir Robin Butler, who told the committee, 'I am in no doubt that it [the story] was impacting on his official position, both his credibility and the attention he could give to his duties as Chancellor if no action was taken.' Questioned as to the sheer amount of money involved, Sir Robin did admit that it was higher than normal 'because of the nature of the exotic calling of the lady'. Sir Terence Burns, who had taken over Sir Peter Middleton's post, stated that it had been necessary to react extremely quickly. 'It was also clear that there was a risk of libellous and dangerous follow-up stories.'[2]

What had also emerged was that the Chancellor had made two omissions. He did not list the gift from the anonymous benefactor in the Register of Members' Interests and nor did he inform the Inland Revenue of his piece of good fortune. According to a statement made by the Inland Revenue,[3] Mr Lamont should have declared the £4,700 of public money he received and paid tax on it unless it was directly connected with his job as Chancellor. He would also be liable for 40 per cent tax, some £7,360, on the anonymous donation. Further, if he or the Treasury had failed to declare the money, he could then face back tax with interest and 100 per cent penalty, the interest to be charged at the then base rate (fixed by the Chancellor) of the Bank of England.

On 18 January 1993, Mr Lamont issued his own statement on the affair and a report that had been carried in the *Guardian* (16.1.93) that the Conservative Party had its own special fund for helping Ministers out of embarrassing difficulties. With regard to the latter he was 'unable to comment', but as to the source of the anonymous gift: 'I did not know anything about where it came from at all.' In answer to criticism that he had employed one of the country's most expensive lawyers, he said, 'It was for dealing with the press inquiries. It started as a private matter, but because of allegations – which I don't wish to repeat – that were made at the time it became a matter that reflected on me in my office.

'It was the judgement not of me, I did not make the decision, but of the head of the Civil Service and the then Permanent Secretary Sir Peter Middleton, and his successor, Sir Terence Burns, that it was appropriate. They were the people who saw what actually happened, what was being alleged, the volume of inquiries that I had to deal with. They decided these costs arose because I was Chancellor of the Exchequer. I did not ask them to make that decision. I never suggested they make that decision. It was their decision themselves.' He found it regrettable that John Smith had raised the issue at Prime Minister's Question Time. Responding to questions regarding what he described as a spate of damaging and inaccurate personal stories about him, he said they were difficult to explain. 'They are a series of coincidences.'

The damaging and inaccurate personal stories had surfaced after the Chancellor's real credibility problem, the traumatic events of what became known as Black Wednesday, the day in September 1992 when, after much macho talk, the pound had been forced out of the European monetary system, the ERM. Mr Lamont's disastrous attempts to stem the collapse of the pound cost taxpayers around £5bn and were rightly described as the most costly mistake ever made in a single day by any Chancellor.

Beside that, the leak to the *Sun* newspaper that the Chancellor was £470 overdrawn on his Access credit card account was pretty small beer, as was the question of whether or not he had bought a bottle of champagne and a packet of cigarettes from a branch of the Threshers off-licence chain. Later the shop assistants at the Paddington branch of Threshers said they had lied and one of them, who was not a British national, was returned to his home country with amazing speed.

Detailed examination of the Chancellor's household budget following the gossip revealed that he was having problems managing on £63,000 per year, what with school fees of around £20,000 a year for his two children, his wife's designer clothes, his taste for expensive restaurants and lavish hospitality. For several months his fellow Ministers closed ranks behind him in the face of increasing calls for his resignation, following the revelations regarding the payments to Peter Carter Ruck. In a comment column in the *Guardian* headed 'If this is the New Ethical Order, it Stinks' (7.1.93), Hugo Young contrasted the case of Norman Lamont with that of a German politician, Jurgen Molleman, who was the Chancellor's counterpart in the German government. Molleman, accused of peddling influence on behalf of a relative of his wife – he had signed blank letters on official notepaper recommending the design of a particular shopping trolley! – admitted that he had been in error and promptly resigned. It took many months for Norman Lamont to follow suit.

'He Did Nothing Illegal. . . .'

On 8 January 1994 MP Alan Duncan, PPS to the then Health Minister, Brian Mawhinney, was enjoying the après-ski hospitality following a day on the Davos pistes. Mr Duncan, who is regularly described as a millionaire, gives his declared interests as owner of Harcourt Consultants, trading as oil broker and adviser on energy matters. Mr Duncan's London home is 18 Gayfere Street, a Georgian house in a Westminster terrace described in the last century as being in a street 'occupied by carriage folk'. He had purchased his house for about £230,000 before being returned as Conservative MP for Rutland and Melton at the 1992 general election. The house had achieved a place in recent history as the 'bunker' used by John Major's campaign team during the 1990 leadership election, but part of its appeal was that it had an extensive wine cellar. After moving in, Mr Duncan installed numerous phone lines and fax machines to assist in his work as an oil broker.

What had attracted attention to Mr Duncan, however, and caused the media to track him down on the slopes, was the charge that he had bought a Council house on the cheap using the government's right-to-buy legislation.

The house in question was No. 17 Gayfere Street, next door to Mr Duncan's home. Unlike No. 18, which had been extensively renovated, No. 17 was somewhat run down, there was no central heating, the roof leaked and there was no proper bathroom. It was being lived in by a retired Liberal Councillor, Harry Ball-Wilson. Mr Ball-Wilson had complained bitterly to his neighbour that he was unable to get Westminster Council to put his house right, after which the two came up with a cunning plan.[4] Under the right-to-buy legislation, Mr Ball-Wilson could buy his house if he had the money. So what was to stop Mr Duncan giving him the money? Mr Ball-Wilson would then live in it rent free until he died, when the property would pass to Mr Duncan. After legal advice had been taken, the property was purchased at a price of £140,000; it was then repaired and modernised, central heating was installed and a new bathroom put in. All would have been well had not Mr Ball-Wilson, who had spent years living on his own, met a lady while on holiday whom he subsequently married. He then moved out of 17 Gayfere Street and let it to a tenant, thus releasing Mr Duncan from the obligation to allow him to live in it until he died. This caused a dilemma, for if it was discovered that the house had been sold within three years of its purchase, then under the right-to-buy scheme, much of the discount would have had to have been refunded. Mr Duncan therefore waited until the three years were up, in June 1994, before registering the fact that he had bought the property from Mr Ball-Wilson.[5]

When the story broke in January 1994 there was a great deal of criticism, it being pointed out that the right-to-buy scheme had not been drawn up with thirty-six-year-old millionaires in mind, even if 'all the financial benefit has gone to the sitting tenant and all the financial expenditure has been mine', as Mr Duncan explained when questioned by the press. He went on to claim that the fall in the property market meant that the house, which might well have risen in value to around £300,000 at the peak of the boom, was probably worth no more by that time than when he had given Mr Ball-Wilson the money with which to buy it.

However, several hours after making the statement, Mr Duncan felt it incumbent on him to resign, which he did, making it clear however that 'there is no question of any impropriety or anything illegal in the transaction I entered into'. In this he was supported by his Minister. Dr Mawhinney said, 'Some years ago, before he entered Parliament, Alan Duncan made some business judgements. My understanding is that he did nothing illegal. He has now judged it right to stand down as my PPS. I was looking forward to working with him, but respect his decision. As far as I am concerned, the matter is closed.'[6]

Single Parents

It was back at the time of the 1983 Conservative Party conference that Ms Sara Keays told the world that she was expecting a baby by Cecil Parkinson. This led, amid much publicity for the Thatcher administration's attachment to Victorian values, to Mr Parkinson's resignation from Cabinet office, although he was later brought back from the cold to become first Energy Secretary, then Transport Secretary. Faced with choosing between the favour of Margaret Thatcher and her wish that he should remain with his wife, and his duty to the expectant Miss Keays, Mr Parkinson chose the former. There was a considerable gap between the Parkinson scandal and Heritage Minister David Mellor's well-publicised affair with actress Antonia de Sancha ten years later. He, too, resigned, not over the allegations of toe-sucking or the Chelsea football strip, but after revelations that he had accepted a free holiday for himself and his family from a female acquaintance. When he went, in September 1993, he blamed the media for forcing him from office. Then there were the revelations in October 1993 that Roads Minister Steven Norris had run a clutch of mistresses simultaneously following the breakdown of his marriage. All the small stuff of gossip columns, maybe, except that in October 1993 John Major had personally launched his Back to Basics campaign at the Conservative Party Conference.

In the wake of a number of embarrassing revelations, government spokespersons attempted to make it clear that Back to Basic decency had not meant, well, *morality* as such, not specific *personal sexual* morality, there had been no intention of picking on human frailty; but it appeared that the electorate in general and Conservative activists in particular were unable to make this nice distinction.

It was, therefore, somewhat unfortunate with hindsight that junior Environment Minister Tim Yeo, MP for Suffolk South, had recently addressed his local branch of what used to be the Marriage Guidance Council and is now known as Relate. 'It is,' he had said, 'in everyone's interests to reduce broken families and the number of single parents. I have seen from my constituency the consequences of marital breakdown.' He was harping on a familiar theme; from the Social Security Secretary Peter Lilley's jokey version of the song from *The Mikado*, 'I've got a little list', at the 1992 Party Conference, to arguments which are still going on, single parents, or rather single mothers, have been blamed for a whole host of today's ills.

It was equally unfortunate that in December 1993 the *News of the World* revealed that Mr Yeo had himself added to the tally of single mothers and was the father of a six-month-old daughter. Following this revelation, Mr Yeo's lawyer, Mr Peter Carter Ruck, issued a statement on his behalf confirming that he was indeed the father of Claudia-Marie, whose mother was solicitor Julia Stent, then a Conservative Councillor in Hackney. Mr Yeo had met Ms Stent during the 1992 Conservative Party Conference and had enjoyed a brief liaison, resulting nine months later in the birth of Claudia-Marie.[7] Mr Yeo himself was unavailable for comment, having fled to the Seychelles after hiding from photographers in the back of his car.

When he did emerge from seclusion to answer his critics it was to say, 'I have acted very foolishly but I don't think my credibility is damaged', a view which it appeared was not shared by his constituency party, who had had no idea of the story that was about to break. While Mr Yeo received support from Party Chairman Sir Norman Fowler, other senior Conservatives soon let it be known that they felt he should have resigned immediately he had learned that the *News of the World* knew of the liaison. Questioned on the BBC on 2 January 1994, however, Mr Yeo chose to tough it out, saying that the government's strictures on one-parent families did not apply to him because he was supporting his daughter financially, the inference being that government criticism had not been levelled at single mothers *per se* but at those whose offspring were not receiving support from errant fathers. Asked if he would resign, Mr Yeo had replied, 'I see no conflict. I believe it has been accepted by my colleagues in government that my conduct has been an entirely private matter. I expected to be judged as a Minister by my performance in office.

'The government's position on family values, which is certainly one I share, is not jeopardised by anything that I have done. I have acted very foolishly in this matter. I would not deny that at all, but I do not believe my credibility as a Minister has been damaged at all. The government has rightly expressed concern about the costs that arise to the taxpayer from a number of single mothers whose financial support derives entirely from the public purse, and that is not the case in this situation.' The clamour for Yeo's resignation grew, alongside criticism that John Major should sack his errant Minister and have done with it. Later, faced with reporters waiting for him outside the Department of the Environment, Mr Yeo emphasised that he still had the 'continued support of the Prime Minister, the Party Chairman and many party colleagues. I am absolutely determined that I and no further Minister will be driven out of office by media pressure.'

However, following outspoken comments by his constituency

party Chair, Patricia Fitzpatrick, and his local members' refusal to support his continuing in office as a Minister, he finally and reluctantly resigned. His tenacious efforts to hang on at almost any cost were, to say the least, undignified compared with the stance of his wife who, among other things, had to care for their two children, both of whom had severe health problems, and that of Ms Stent, who refused every incentive to make a financial killing from selling her story to the media.

Not a Penny More, Not a Penny Less

On Friday 8 July 1994 *The Times* ran a front-page lead story which had come to them as a result of a leak. It was headed 'Shares Inquiry on Jeffrey Archer'. Following representations made by *The Times* consequent upon that leak, the Department of Trade and Industry had confirmed to the paper that it was investigating an allegation of insider trading concerning Jeffrey, now Lord, Archer, and the purchase and sale of Anglia Television shares. Insider trading is illegal.

The initial story was brief. On 18 January 1994 Labour peer Lord Hollick, Chairman of the communications group MAI, had launched a £292m takeover bid for Anglia TV. The news sent share prices soaring. Throughout 1993 Anglia shares had doubled in value due to constant rumours of possible takeovers, but the confirmation of the Hollick bid resulted in Anglia shares gaining a further 180p a share, until they finally stood at a staggering 664p each. It was during this period, it was claimed, that Lord Archer had purchased and sold shares in Anglia TV.

The Times immediately contacted Lord Archer, who vigorously denied the story. 'It is completely untrue,' he said. 'I did not buy any shares. I am not going to make a statement. That sort of accusation is libellous. Thank you.'[8]

The *Times* story could not have come at a less welcome time for Lord Archer, as he was currently being widely tipped either for the post of Conservative Party Chairman, which he had made no secret of wanting, or being brought into government as Heritage Minister. This has, not surprisingly, led to endless speculation as to who leaked the story about the DTI at that particular moment and why. So far no one has come forward and confessed.

However, hard on the heels of the *Times* report, Michael Heseltine, in his capacity as President of the Board of Trade, announced on 28 July that his officials had finished their inquiry into the allegations of insider trading, that he had studied their report and had concluded that his officials 'should take no further action against any of the parties concerned'. Lord Archer immediately announced that he had been 'exonerated'.

Lord Archer is, as everyone knows, a multi-million pound best-selling author, listed among the 500 wealthiest people in Britain with a fortune estimated at around £25m. He took up fiction after losing £270,000 in the Canadian company Aquablast Incorporated. It later transpired he had been the unwitting victim of a Mafia-backed share swindle. The big financial loss almost bankrupted him and caused him to resign from his seat as Conservative MP for Louth.

Controversy has followed Jeffrey Archer ever since. Thirteen years later, in 1986, he was accused in the *Daily Star* of offering, through an associate, £2,000 to a prostitute, Monica Coughlan, who had been threatening to publish details of an alleged association. Archer sued for libel and won £500,000. The trial was notable not least for the extraordinary behaviour of the judge, Mr Justice Caulfield, who, after hearing Mary Archer's evidence of her husband's fidelity, waxed lyrical in his summing up. She was 'elegant', even 'fragrant'. 'Remember Mary Archer,' he drooled, 'your vision of her will never disappear.' It was widely felt by many observers that Mary Archer's evidence had helped win her husband the case. As ever, Lord Archer bounced back, even surviving a savage piece by Ian Jack in the *London Review of Books*, which, following intense discussion among journalists as to the many conflicting facts in Lord Archer's CV, set about researching it. Jack described Archer as a fantasist who made up details of his birth, schooling, university education and his father's job and heroism during the last war. This story continued in true serial fashion when the media discovered during the summer of

1994 that Lord Archer had an unknown half-sister and an older half-brother, also called Jeffrey.

Within days of the original story breaking, Lord Archer's wife, Mary, was also in the news, as throughout the negotiations for the Anglia takeover she was a non-executive director of Anglia TV.

Slowly and painfully through the summer of 1994 the details of the remarkable share transaction dribbled out. The tale begins on 31 December 1993, when Anglia's Chairman, Sir Peter Gibbings, sent Lady Archer two sets of highly confidential memoranda regarding four proposed takeover bids for the company. She and her fellow directors were also provided with a document, *Anglia – Strategic Options*, drawn up by the company's bankers S. G. Warburg on the same day. The documents showed that Lord Hollick's MAI group had submitted their takeover bid on 16 December 1993.[9]

On 5 January 1994 members of the Anglia board met to discuss the Hollick bid. They met again on 12 January, a meeting attended by Lady Archer, and were told that MAI was offering 610p per share. After discussing the offer it was agreed that the company should hold out for a better share price. Later that night at an informal meeting, Sir Peter and Lord Hollick agreed a share price of 640p plus an interim dividend at 10p per share, subject to the approval of Hollick's own board. On 13 January 1994 all Anglia directors, including Lady Archer, were informed that there would be a full board meeting on the following Sunday.[10]

It was on 13 January that Lord Archer rang a firm of stock-brokers, Charles Stanley, whom he had never used before, and asked them to buy 50,000 Anglia shares at the then price of 485p each. The firm came back to Lord Archer and told him that only 25,000 were available that day, whereupon Lord Archer agreed to buy what there was. He then informed Charles Stanley that the shares were to be purchased in the name of Broosk Fawzi Saib. Mr Saib is a Kurdish friend of Lord Archer and a member of a wealthy Iraqi family. According to the *Observer* Mr Saib had had a run of financial bad luck when the two first met in 1992. Mr Saib has lived in Britain since 1985, although until 1990 he used the surname 'Jamal'. He was in partnership with two others when his business went into liquidation in 1991, owing £149,000. A second business, Broosk Estate Agents, set up in 1986, collapsed at the same time with debts of £71,000. For two years in the late 1980s Mr Saib also ran London Construction and Design, which collapsed in 1994. He appears, however, to have been a seasoned buyer and seller of shares in his own right.[11]

On 14 January Lord Archer was back on the phone to Charles Stanley for another 25,000 shares at 485p each. According to all those who have investigated the matter, including the *Financial Times* (18.8.94), Lord Archer asked for the whole transaction to be completed within the next stock exchange fortnightly accounting period. This is known as a 'new account' deal and actually costs more money to set up, but it has definite advantages. The whole deal as it stood could have cost Lord Archer nearly £250,000. If, however, the shares were resold within the fortnight no cash would have to change hands at all. Again Lord Archer asked for the shares to be purchased in the name of Broosk Saib.

On 16 January the Anglia directors, including Lady Archer, attended a board meeting at the offices of S. G. Warburg in the City, when the MAI bid was formally agreed. Minutes of that meeting show that Lady Archer, along with everyone else attending it, was reminded of her legal responsibilities under the City takeover code in a letter from Anglia's lawyers, Linklaters and Paines. One requirement is that all information regarding such a bid must be kept strictly confidential. Another is that directors must undertake to inform 'connected persons' that they had an obligation to disclose any possible share deals regarding the relevant company. In fact Anglia directors had been told that before, back in 1992, when they had been asked to confirm by letter that they fully understood this requirement. It is not known whether or not Lady Archer passed the information on to her husband.

On 18 January the MAI was publicly announced, sending Anglia shares up 180p a share to 664p. In no time Lord Archer was back on the telephone to Charles Stanley instructing him to sell. The cheque for the subsequent profit was to be made out to Mr Saib, but sent to Lord Archer's home.

Within hours Charles Stanley's own team which monitors share transactions reported their concern that there had apparently been a large and unusual share movement. The information was passed on to the Stock Exchange insider trader group, which then passed on its own findings to the DTI. In February 1994 the DTI appointed two inspectors to investigate the possibility of insider trading. At about the same time a cheque for £80,000, duly made out to Mr Saib, was posted to Lord Archer's home. And there the mattered slumbered until the revelation in *The Times* on 8 July.

It is entirely thanks to the tenacity of financial journalists that the story came out at all in such detail: that and the original anonymous leak to *The Times*. Meanwhile Lord Archer, one of the band of Tory politicians known as the rentaquote tendency, was unusually silent. He was on a book promotion tour of Australia which would be followed by a lengthy holiday. Lady Archer, meanwhile, strenuously denied that she had at any time discussed the matter of the Anglia takeover with her husband. At the time of writing she had not been asked to leave the Anglia board; indeed the board issued a statement to the effect that it accepted her reassurance that she had not made public any confidential information.

It is hardly surprising that the saga provided Opposition politicians with a field day, not least Labour Shadow Trade and Industry spokesman Robin Cook who had, in cricketing parlance, been left as his party's nightwatchman during the holiday period. He announced that there were a number of questions to which he would like answers, not least why Lord Archer had been so charitable as to make the purchase for a friend who was himself well used to buying and selling shares, and why the cheque was then sent not to Mr Saib but to Lord Archer. Mr Cook also demanded that the DTI inspectors' report be released. If it did 'exonerate' Lord Archer, as he had claimed, then that would kill the matter once and for all.[12] Mr Cook also expressed his concern that as matters stood 'we have here one top Tory politician sitting in judgement on another top Tory politician – who is celebrated as a friend and supporter of the Prime Minister – and then concluding there are no grounds for further proceedings. The rest of us can be forgiven for asking whether this is the most rigorous way of arriving at an unbiased outcome.' As at the time of writing, Michael Heseltine has resolutely refused to publish the report on the grounds that it would be illegal to do so.

On the evening of 24 August, Lord Archer publicly admitted that he had made 'a grave error'. Not, as might be thought, in actually buying and selling the shares or indeed telling *The Times* that he had never bought any shares in the first place. No, the 'public apology' was to Lady Archer for causing her 'needless embarrassment'. He made no direct comment regarding details of the share deal nor about what happened to the £80,000 estimated profit on the transaction.

The full statement, issued on his behalf by his lawyers, reads, 'There have been no new facts mentioned by the media which were not known to (repeat not known to) and which had not been investigated by the inspectors in the course of their very full inquiry. The DTI who had the inspectors' report before them have stated in their decision that they have taken independent legal advice and have decided that no further action be taken against anyone involved in the inquiry.

'They can accordingly be taken to have concluded that, as Lord Archer has maintained throughout, this transaction was not carried out with the benefit of any insider information.

'He realises, however, that it was a grave error when his wife was a director of Anglia to have allowed his name to be associated with the purchase of the sale of shares in that company on behalf of a third party (and from which he in no way benefited) and indeed his deepest regret is the embarrassment needlessly caused to Lady Archer in this matter.'

The apology raised as many questions as it sought to quell, not least why Lord Archer could not have apologised to Lady Archer in private if that was all he was worried about. Among many questions raised were why had he not used his own regular stockbroker instead of going to a company with which he had never traded before? Why did he buy shares for Saib who had all the necessary expertise to buy his own? Why did he insist the deal was done on a 'new account' basis, if not on the assumption that the shares could be resold within the fortnight at a profit? It would have been very expensive had that not been the case and extra charges would also have had to be found. If things had gone amiss, who would then have footed the bill for over £242,500 on settlement day? Did Mr Saib, with all his business problems, have this kind of money?

On 28 August 1994 Michael Gillard in the *Observer* pointed out that back in 1985 Lord Archer had bought shares in another company which was the subject of a takeover bid, when he purchased £1.5m-worth of shares in the Debenham stores group just before its successful takeover by Burtons. Afterwards the Stock Exchange mounted an investigation into all share transactions which had taken place before and during the takeover, but subsequently took no action.

Chapter 11

THE SLEAZE FACTOR

What is so disturbing about the atmosphere of sleaze is that it now seems to permeate almost all aspects of public life like a dank mist. There is hardly a nook or cranny free of it. Previous chapters have dealt with various aspects of the subject. This one offers a cross-section of examples drawn from a variety of different sources but all contributing to the general picture.

Parliamentary Procedure

It is not only the sight of Honourable Members with their noses in the financial trough that has caused the current climate of intense cynicism. It is the whole way our supposed democratic process operates.

The bi-weekly parliamentary exercise known as Prime Minister's Question Time could now more justly be indexed under entertainment rather than politics. Those who follow the exchange on television or radio can be forgiven if they do not realise that these sessions are supposed to enable ordinary MPs to question the Prime Minister directly on matters of public interest. Firstly, it is now a trial of strength between the Prime Minister and the Leader of the Opposition where both try to score points over each other; this reached its nadir during the Thatcher regime.

Secondly, it has become an arena for the asking of sycophantic and time-wasting questions by MPs, designed to allow the Prime Minister to tell the world how wonderful everything is. Here is Colin Shepherd, Conservative MP for Hereford, on 10 May 1994: 'During the course of a busy day, will my Right Honourable Friend reflect on the fact that over the past year industrial output rose by 3.7 per cent. Will he confirm that it is still possible to publish good news in this country?' John Major: 'Good news is certainly allowed but I fear it may often be masked by less important matters these days. . . .'[1]

Step forward Sir Fergus Montgomery, Conservative MP for Altincham and Sale and director of Messenger Television Productions and Clos-O-Mat (GB) Ltd, and consultant to Welbeck Public Relations Ltd, National Association of Bookmakers and National Breakdown. He is asking a question, also on 10 May 1994, the answer to which will obviously stun the nation: 'Can the Prime Minister give an assurance that the government and the police will give top priority to tackling the drug barons and the vice trade?' John Major: 'Yes, I can certainly give my Honourable Friend that assurance.'[2]

Nine days later, on 19 May 1994, Simon Burns, Conservative MP for Chelmsford and adviser to Scope Communications Management Ltd, McDonalds, Toyota, W. H. Smith, Rank Xerox, Halfords and Allied Lyons, asked, 'Does my Right Honourable Friend agree that the unemployment figures and steady fall in unemployment over the past twelve months is welcome news which shows that our economic recovery is steady and sustainable?' John Major: 'My Honourable Friend makes a telling point with great clarity.'[3] On 15 June 1994 Ian Bruce, Conservative MP for South Dorset and adviser to Telecommunications Managers Association, Trevor Gilbert and Associates (a division of Recruitment Network Ltd) and recipient of free satellite and services from British Sky Broadcasting, a free holiday in 1993 at the invitation of Centre Parcs, two free fax machines from Southern Electricity plc and a gift of mobile telephone equipment from Talkland International UK Ltd, put his question to the Prime Minister. 'Has my Right Honourable Friend seen that unemployment fell by 10 per cent in my constituency in the past quarter? Is it not a tribute to my constituents' positive attitudes to job creation and their refusal to take strike action?' John Major: 'My Honourable Friend is entirely right about that.'[4]

These are just a selection out of hundreds of similar questions, all of which take up the very brief amount of time allowed and which help to ensure that real questions requiring real answers never get heard.

Nicholas Scott and the Disablement Bill

Nor is this time the only misuse of parliamentary procedure. The talking out of Bills so that they cannot be passed is an old, if not an honourable, tradition. One of the most recent examples is that of the Private Members' Bill put forward by the Labour MP for Kingswood, Dr Roger Berry, with the aim of giving more rights to the disabled. The whole business of getting a Private Members' Bill before the House is, literally, a lottery, with MPs' names being drawn out of a hat. Even if an MP comes out near the top of the draw and thus has parliamentary time made available to him or her, the hurdles which a Bill has to surmount make it a rare occurrence for it to proceed any further and it is almost bound to fail if a government disagrees with its premise. In the case of Dr Berry's Bill, although it had cross-party support, the government was against it right from the start, claiming – against all the relevant financial statistics – that it would cost £18m to implement.

This Bill, which only called for disabled people to be given the same statutory rights as women and ethnic minorities, actually got as far as its committee stage, where there was ample time for those against to raise objections, but when it came before the House in May 1994 for its second reading, it was suddenly swamped by no fewer than eighty amendments put forward by four Conservative MPs, who talked it out. Called to account, Nicholas Scott, the Minister for the Disabled, told the House that the government had not sought to block the Bill, nor had any of his civil servants helped draft the amendments.

But this contradicted a statement made later by Leader of the

House Tony Newton, that government lawyers had advised on the amendments used to talk the Bill out. A few days later in a letter to Labour MP Dale Campbell-Savours, Mr Scott admitted that what he had told the House had been 'incorrect'. The government had wanted its concerns over the Bill voiced, 'and I therefore authorised my officials to approach Parliamentary Counsel with a request that he should prepare some draft amendments. In the event, given the government's view that it was not practical to turn the Bill into a viable statute through amendment, it was judged more appropriate to hand the amendments to government backbenchers with similar concerns.' The four MPs had claimed the amendments were all their own work.

As a result of the letter Mr Scott had to make a humiliating personal statement to the House in which he admitted that what he had told MPs during the debate on the Bill had not been correct. He continued to insist, however, that his officials had not actually drafted the amendments but only helped with their preparation: 'I very much regret that by not giving a fuller explanation at the time the effect of my reply was misleading and I offer my unreserved apologies to the House.'

The late John Smith, in his capacity as Leader of the Opposition, at once wrote to the Prime Minister demanding that Mr Scott be made to resign. Yet, in spite of the fact that John Major himself had written in a letter only a month previously that Ministers who knowingly failed to give accurate information should go, he stood firmly by his Minister. A statement issued from Downing Street said that the circumstances did not warrant Mr Scott's departure and that so far as the Prime Minister was concerned, the matter was at an end.

On 12 May 1994 John Smith died suddenly from a heart attack, by which time Dr Berry had managed to salvage enough of his Bill to bring it before the Commons once again. The day chosen was 20 May, that of John Smith's funeral, when government organisers assumed that virtually every Labour MP would be in Scotland attending it. Government whips were confident, therefore, that the Bill could be kept out of the Commons. However, a small group of Labour MPs, determined that the Bill should be passed, agreed not to go to Scotland and arrived to debate it, resulting in

Mr Scott being forced to turn up and talk out the Bill himself. This actually led Tory MP Terry Dicks to call him a liar, a statement which, like others before him, he had to withdraw for, you must understand, Honourable Members never lie. . . . Mr Scott again claimed the legislation would cost £18m, but even his own backbenchers described the figure as 'bogus' and knowingly based on an outdated premise.

In a final effort to get the Bill through the Commons, Dr Berry had actually agreed a whole raft of government amendments, yet Scott read from a prepared text ignoring completely the fact that many of the reasons he put forward for rejecting the Bill had been dealt with by the acceptance of the amendments.

Nor was the Minister alone in misleading the House. Lady Olga Maitland, Conservative MP for Sutton and Cheam and a constant spokesperson on law and order, had to make not one but two apologies to the House (the first not being accepted by the Speaker) for insisting that she had not received any assistance in drawing up her amendments to the Bill, after which she appeared on television newscasts giving the impression that she felt she had done nothing wrong.

In the aftermath, it was claimed in the *Observer* (22.5.94) that Scott had, in fact, tried to resign after his apology to the House, but had been told not to, in order to protect the Prime Minister. When news got around that resignation was in the air, Social Security Secretary Peter Lilley, Leader of the House Tony Newton and Chief Whip Richard Ryder argued against it, fearing, according to 'a senior government source', that 'without Mr Scott there would be no one to shield the Prime Minister, who had been dithering for weeks before deciding the Bill must be killed'. According to the source, Mr Scott had actually tried to persuade Ministers to accept the Bill, suitably amended, and he had had Mr Lilley on his side, but he had been vigorously opposed by Michael Heseltine, President of the Board of Trade, and the then Employment Secretary, David Hunt. The government, the source continued, had known for weeks that the Bill was coming up 'but nobody could get a decision out of the Prime Minister over whether it should be amended or blocked'. In John Major's July reshuffle, Mr Scott lost his job.

On 12 August Sir Robin Butler, Cabinet Secretary and head of the Home Civil Service admitted in a letter to Labour MP Mike O'Brien that civil servants had indeed drafted amendments for six Bills between 1993 and 1994 and may well have helped with far more. The Bills were the Medicines Information Bill (1993), the Osteopaths Bill (1993), the Right to Know Bill (1993), the Chiropractors Bill (1993), the Energy Conservation Bill (1993) and the Race Relations Remedies Bill (1994). He also added that civil servants had been involved in the preparation of amendments for six Bills during the Labour administration of 1974–79.

Sir Robin refused to say if there had been other occasions when this had occurred, on the grounds that it would be wrong in that he could only reveal such involvement when the government itself was also willing to acknowledge that it had taken place. He wrote, 'I cannot indicate whether or not amendments were intended to wreck a Bill, even if that were clear in the papers. There may be an understandable difference of view between the supporters of a Bill and others on that point. But I would not be giving any secrets away if I said there had been complaints from MPs that both Conservative and Labour governments have used various means to prevent Private Members' Bills becoming law.'

There is now growing disquiet about the influence wielded by the increasing number of individual Parliamentary lobbyists and lobby companies. On 12 May 1994 reports appeared in the media that Central Television had cancelled an edition of *The Cook Report* which investigated links between lobbyists and MPs acting as consultants and advisers to such companies.

Special attention had been paid to one of the largest companies, Ian Greer Associates. In the programme – details of which were widely reported in the press – Mr Greer had claimed easy access to the Parliamentary Private Secretaries of John Major and Michael Portillo, along with former Chancellor Norman Lamont and the then junior DTI Minister, Neil Hamilton. *The Cook Report* had set up a bogus company, Ecocon Ventures, purporting to be run by former Russian communists now wanting to buy up a privatised British agency of some kind. According to David Hencke in the *Guardian*, Mr Greer also offered a list of fourteen Conservative

MPs he could draw on for assistance, and said he could produce details of a confidential report on the privatisation of the Insolvency Services currently being prepared for Ministers which he said had come direct from senior civil servants at the DTI.

Interviews shown in the programme, made before the cash-for-questions affair surfaced, appeared to show Mr Greer speaking of being able to talk to Ministers at the highest level. The idea for the programme had come from reports of earlier investigations into the activities of lobbyists. It was also claimed that the introduction of 'Ecocon' to Ian Greer Associates had been undertaken by Sir Michael Grylls, MP for Surrey South West. Immediately before the programme was stopped, Mr Greer had sent a copy of a four-page analysis of a confidential report by Stoy Hayward Consulting to 'Ecocon' on the privatisation of the Insolvency Service, giving a detailed breakdown of what was likely to be offered for sale and the timetable set by Ministers.

The reluctant publicity shone a spotlight on Mr Greer and his strong links with the Conservative Party. Indeed, in 1993 he had paid for the fringe conference agenda sent to 5,000 delegates at Blackpool. He also paid £5,000 to have John Major's speeches collected and published by the Conservative Political Centre, after Central Office had been unable to find industrial sponsors. He provided John Major with a car and chauffeur during his bid to become party leader, and during the 1992 general election he allowed Norman Lamont to use his detached house in Kingston 'for rest and recuperation'. In his youth Ian Greer was the youngest Tory agent to be appointed by Central Office. His salary is reputed to be in the region of £300,000 a year and he has a division bell in his offices in St Catherine's Place to enable MPs and Ministers attending his various functions to rush back to the House to vote, even going so far as to lay on taxis to get them there in time. His clients have included British Gas, British Airways, Coca-Cola, Cadbury Schweppes, the governments of Malaysia, Pakistan, Taiwan and Brazil and, oddly, the African National Congress.[6]

A week after the reports surfaced in the press, Ian Greer wrote to three Labour MPs, Nigel Griffiths, Paul Flynn and Angela Eagle, stating that 'the full Phase One Report on privatisation by Stoy

Hayward is not publicly available. We did not, nor would we expect to, have access to it. However, the summary of Phase One is available to the public at the DTI's library, Ashdown House. It was there a researcher was allowed to see a summary from which she took notes.' Yet the *Guardian* insists that two days after the visit to the library, Mr Greer had still been unable to supply the necessary information to Ecocon and that Jeremy Sweeney, Greer's Managing Director, had written to Ecocon saying it was necessary to ensure the report went far deeper than 'simply what is currently available and a number of senior civil servants that we have needed to talk to have not been available'. Mr Greer himself said in his letter enclosing his report that he had gone to considerable lengths to research and include information 'not yet in the public domain'. This leads to the conclusion that if the information was truly fully available to the public, then Mr Greer was being paid for something anyone could find out, and that if it wasn't, then someone had leaked it to him.

The story of Ecocon is the tip of an iceberg. Many people both inside and outside Parliament are concerned at the influence of lobbyists on policy, influence which often far exceeds that of ordinary voters. Efforts to allow MPs to see *The Cook Report* continued unavailingly throughout the summer, leading Alan Williams, Labour MP for Swansea West, to conclude, 'It is utterly unacceptable. It is possible that the material would be of great interest to the Committee on Members' Interests and Privileges.'

The Pergau Dam Affair

This story beings in 1988 when the then British Defence Secretary George, now Lord, Younger visited Malaysia to negotiate an arms deal. While there it appears he gave what is described in Mandarinese as a 'reassurance' that Malaysia was eligible for British aid. For reasons which remain unclear, Lord Younger did not feel it necessary to check with the Foreign Office before giving the nod to the Malaysian government. What the Malaysian government wanted was aid – to the tune of £417m – to build a massive dam, a scheme which remains deeply controversial. What Lord Younger wanted was a £1bn arms deal. Arms-for-aid deals are illegal.

For four and a half years MPs questioned what seemed to be a dark deal, not least when it was discovered that, by the oddest of coincidences, two letters had been sent from London to Kuala Lumpur on the same day, one confirming the arms deal and the other confirming the aid. These two letters, it was argued, 'broke the link' between the giving of aid and the buying of arms.

Matters came to a head in the winter of 1993–94, not least when *The Sunday Times* published details of the link between the aid and arms, a story which led to the Malaysian government threatening to withdraw all trade links with Britain unless our government restrained our press. It might be added that a number of Conservative backbench MPs went along with this view on the grounds that the media were trying to destroy jobs.

Faced with growing pressure, the government finally asked the House of Commons Committee on Foreign Affairs to look into the matter. The committee's findings, conveniently published after Parliament had risen for its fourteen-week summer holiday, make interesting reading. Getting to the nub of it all is difficult, but it seems that the crunch came in 1991 when the Overseas Development Administration raised sound and realistic objections to the whole Pergau Dam project, not only on grounds of cost – and this was to be one of the most costly aid packages ever offered by Britain – but on those of its utility and effect on the environment.

But there was a problem. Mrs Thatcher herself, when Prime Minister, had nursed along the arms deal. So it was that John Major and Douglas Hurd overruled the ODA, as it was 'felt we must honour Mrs Thatcher's word'. Douglas Hurd explained that he 'had to take a wider perspective' on the matter as there would be 'grievous consequences' for British business if Britain reneged on its aid offer. As the *Guardian* commented in its leader on 21 July 1994, 'On such grounds of principle was this unprincipled deal confirmed.'

The Foreign Affairs Committee castigates the failure of the

Ministry of Defence to inform or consult the Foreign Office over its arms-for-aid link. Lord Younger comes in for particular criticism over his handling of the deals which led to what the Committee described as Mrs Thatcher's and John Major's 'moral obligation' to back the dam project. British companies with an interest in the Pergau scheme were also criticised for putting pressure on Mrs Thatcher to approve it.

The report says, 'We consider it reprehensible for the Ministry of Defence to have prepared for, and conducted, negotiations with another country in 1988 without specific reference to the Foreign and Commonwealth Office as soon as it was known that the other party wished to add to those talks a dimension falling within the FCO's remit.

'We are particularly concerned that this should have occurred in relation to such a sensitive issue as a conditional linkage between development aid and defence sales, which was contrary to stated government policy.' Veiled criticism is levelled at Mrs Thatcher and ex-Overseas Aid Minister Chris Patten for failing to keep Parliament properly informed when answering MP's questions. 'Ministerial replies were literally true, though less open and informative than the House has a right to expect.' Lady Thatcher, in her capacity as ex-Prime Minister, had refused to give evidence to the committee and committee members split on party lines as to whether or not her answers would have shown if she had turned a blind eye to the arms-for-aid deal.

Yet many MPs simply failed to see what all the fuss was about. Rules are made to be broken, what is wrong with getting something back in return for an aid deal? And, after all, Britain is the world's sixth largest arms dealer. The committee concluded that supposed reforms to prevent other arms-for-aid deals do not go far enough.

Setting a Good Example

As part of the economy drive on public spending, student grants were frozen in 1987 at approximately £45 a week. At the same time students were told they could no longer apply for housing benefit to help them pay rent. Students who would suffer hardship as a result, and this particularly applied to those from poorer homes and to mature students, would be able to get loans instead. For some time the government touted its idea around the major clearing banks with little success. Finally, therefore, yet another Quango, the Student Loans Company, was set up to administer the scheme. Students, finding themselves on a grant which fell steadily in real terms, while also having to pay rent, the whole compounded by a recession which made holiday jobs almost unobtainable, took advantage of the meagre loans on offer in large numbers.

By the end of the 1993–94 academic year it was clear that many students had simply been unable to repay their loans and it was widely publicised that the Student Loans Company would be pursuing defaulters vigorously for the recovery of taxpayers' money.

In September 1994 Labour MP Stephen Byers was leaked a fascinating dossier from the Department of Education which showed that those administering the loans scheme were certainly setting an example. It was illuminating to note what the Students Loans Company deemed to be legitimate expenses – tickets for pop concerts, gifts of perfume and whisky, corporate credit cards, even an expensive celebratory lunch and all generously paid for by us, the taxpayers. The company's Chief Executive, Ron Harrison, has been particularly well looked after. Due to retire in 1995, he has generously been awarded by the Treasury a 17.5 per cent increase in his pension. It would seem, too, that the Student Loans Company is founding a dynasty, for Mr Harrison's son Barry was not only employed by the company but used its staff to help him move house.[7]

The authors of the dossier say, 'The company has acknowledged an infringement here. Of itself it must be regarded as a relatively minor matter, although the company accepts that it sets the wrong tone and must not happen again.'

It was as a result of two anonymous letters to the Education Department that a fraud investigation was mounted into the affairs of the company and the department's internal auditors were called in. The internal auditors say that they found no evidence of corruption, but they did question whether or not what went on broke Whitehall guidelines. One senior manager was sacked for incompetence.

It is interesting to note that the dossier was not shown to the House of Commons Public Accounts Committee when it investigated the company in 1993. It obviously should have been. £82.80 was spent on tickets for a Dire Straits concert, £30 on perfume for Japanese visitors, £110 on gifts of Marks and Spencer vouchers and £61.80 on cigars. In two months in 1992 Mr Harrison spent £350 on spirits for his boardroom. The petty cash bill for whisky alone totalled £252. Hospitality for entertainment at a cricket match reached £470. We also paid for Mr Harrison to take his wife and secretary out to lunch at an exclusive hotel on the shores of Loch Lomond, the outing being by chauffeur-driven car. Apparently Mr Harrison organised the excursion as a birthday treat for his secretary, taking his wife along for what he described to the auditors as 'reasons which he hopes are obvious'. Nor was Mr Harrison's chauffeur neglected. He was allowed to use one of the firm's cars to take his wife and family on holiday on the reasonable grounds that 'while Mr Conway and his family have two cars, neither would have provided similar accommodation for the family and luggage'.

Concern continues that a whiff of nepotism might still hang in the air. The Public Accounts Committee, belatedly shown a copy of the dossier, responded, 'The report does not entirely dispel the suspicion of nepotism surrounding the recruitment of Mr Barry Harrison by a manager, Ted Brophy, who had previously worked with and been helped by Mr Ron Harrison before they joined the company and who appears to owe his current job to Mr Ron Harrison. For internal audit to say that they were not interested in the previous association of these two men seems naïve.' Mr Brophy has had an exciting life, having been kidnapped by the IRA and had his car used for a murder at the time he was working for Mr Harrison. According to David Hencke in the *Guardian*, he was offered the job after it was considered no suitable applicants had responded to advertisements for his post.[8]

Mr Byers has now sent the dossier to the National Audit Office and inquiries into the running of the Student Loan Company have been reopened.

The Politicising of the Civil Service

An edition of the *Observer* on 29 April 1994 carried a statement attributed to a Whitehall press office which is worth quoting:

'The administration has been in power for fifteen years, and it's inevitable that, where black used to meet white, you can get grey areas developing. A few years ago you might have said, "Stop, I can't do that, it breaks all the civil service rules." That's become less and less easy. Nowadays you end up finding ways to break those rules instead.

'We're not supposed to be party political, but we are. We send out press notices which are fundamentally political. They ought to come from Central Office instead, if we were obeying the rules.' The spokesman gives a possible example. An Opposition MP ('Mr X') puts down lots of embarrassing parliamentary questions attacking a Minister. The media want a response. Rules say the relevant Minister should be tracked down, 'but we're more likely to draft out a quote on his behalf, which will inevitably be pure party politics, instead of just the facts, which is all we're supposed to give out. If we have to put it out on paper, we use unheaded paper, because the Opposition would accuse us, quite rightly, of abusing the department to make politics. We might go further when a journalist rings up, and we might tell him in no uncertain terms that Mr X is a complete bastard, who doesn't know what he's talking about.'

Mr Pink and the Insolvency Service

In April 1994 the Public Accounts Committee published a damning report on the record of the government's Insolvency Service (the agency 'Ecocon' purported to want to buy!) and Companies

House, heavily criticising both over failures to handle a record 153,000 corporate and personal bankruptcies over a three-year period, and the failure of the Insolvency Service to secure more than 1,712 disqualifications of directors, after identifying unfit conduct among 43,000. According to the Public Accounts Committee no fewer than 6,400 should have been disqualified.

On 16 August 1994 the *Guardian* revealed that a senior accountant working for the Insolvency Service was touting for business from companies which might face investigation. The official, Philip Pink, who used to be Deputy Inspector-General of the service and was currently working in its Disqualification Unit (which decides which directors should be considered unfit to continue in post), had sent out a brochure on behalf of his own private company offering 'confidential discussions' on how firms in trouble could be helped to cope with visits from the service. Mr Pink apparently sympathised with companies whose affairs might be investigated and therefore 'in response, I seek to offer you a confidential review from the outcome and implementation of which you should face any such visit with added confidence and reassurance drawn from the viewpoint of an external consultant with considerable experience in the field'.

Warning his recipients that they could face unlimited fines, suspension and disqualification if things went amiss for them, he added, 'This is where the monitoring visit review service offered by Philip Pink and Co will help.' As a reference, Mr Pink pointed out that he had been Deputy Inspector-General of the department for nine years, with responsibilities in the DTI for insolvency policy and new legislation, culminating in the development of the 1986 Insolvency Act.

Contacted by the *Guardian*, Mr Pink expressed extreme annoyance, stating that he was not doing anything against his current contract. He was merely seeking business for when that contract might come to an end. Keith Ellis, Chairman of the Institution of Professional Managerial Staff's Insolvency Unit branch said, 'The government seems to be seconding all sorts of people to work here rather than employ permanent staff. It is currently spending over £1m offering contract jobs to people like Mr Pink.' The DTI was unavailable for comment.

The Scott Inquiry

All the foregoing, even the Pergau Dam scandal, pale into insignificance before what has become known as the arms-to-Iraq affair, a matter of such enormity that it has led to a year-long investigation by Mr Justice Scott, the results of which are not now expected before the spring of 1995 at the earliest. It can only be dealt with in the briefest terms here.

The Scott Inquiry was set up in 1992 after the collapse of the trial of Paul Henderson and two other executives of the Matrix Churchill company who had been accused of supplying arms-related goods to Iraq in contravention of the government's arms embargo, instituted in 1985 at the height of the Iraq-Iran conflict. Mr Henderson's defence, similar to that in another case involving the supply of parts which might have been destined for use in military hardware, was that not only had the government connived at what had gone on but that he himself had been keeping MI6 informed of his actions throughout. During the trial, documents came to light which suggested there had been a secret and deliberate policy to supply Iraq with such defence-related equipment, a policy which had gone on almost up to the start of the Gulf War. It was an emotive issue. We may well, under the auspices of Mrs Thatcher, have supplied arms that were then used against our own troops.

Mr Henderson's defence lawyers called for relevant information from Michael Heseltine, Malcolm Rifkind, Kenneth Clarke and William Waldegrave. The documents were not forthcoming. On the advice of the Attorney General, Sir Nicholas Lyell, all relevant documents were suppressed on the grounds of national security, the Ministers going so far as to sign Public Interest Immunity (PII) certificates to prevent disclosure. Had the trial judge not overruled the Ministers and demanded the documents be produced, Mr Henderson and his colleagues would almost certainly have gone down for long jail sentences.

Rumours of the breaking of the arms embargo were circulating before the Matrix Churchill trial. In March 1990, following the execution by Iraq of *Observer* journalist Farzad Batoft, who had been accused of spying, Opposition spokesmen had urged the government to reconsider its extensive trade credits with Iraq, to which Foreign Secretary Douglas Hurd had replied, 'We must take into account that economic measures in which we will not be joined by others will not alter the stance of the Iraq government and might do more harm than good.' Two weeks later, nuclear detonators bound for Iraq were seized by Customs at Heathrow. In answer to further questions Mr Hurd replied, 'We do not supply arms to Iraq and I am glad to make that clear,' continuing, 'Exports of nuclear technology and arms are covered by the restrictions I mentioned. It is clear from yesterday's events that those are effectively policed and will contine to be.' In January 1992 a book by Kenneth Timmerman, *The Death Lobby,* claimed that Defence Minister Alan Clark had told worried suppliers of tools to Iraq that 'the intended use of machines should be couched in such a manner as to emphasise the peaceful use to which they will be put'. Immediately prior to the collapse of the Matrix Churchill trial, Clark had confirmed on oath that this had indeed been the case.

Month by month, week by week, throughout the autumn of 1993 and half of 1994, a procession of senior civil servants, past and present, and government and former government Ministers has appeared before Mr Scott in public, along with members of the secret service whose evidence has been given in camera. Highlights have included Alan Clark referring to himself as being 'economical with the actualité', a reference to Sir Robert Armstrong who was 'economical with the truth'; Sir Nicholas Lyell changing his mind as to whether or not Ministers had had no option but to sign PII documents; Michael Heseltine's evidence that he had expressed grave reservations about so doing and had asked the Attorney General to pass these on to the Court and that Sir Nicholas had failed to do so; damning evidence from former civil servants; an emotional outburst from Lord Howe leading him to accuse Lord Scott of acting as prosecutor, judge and jury in the affair; and Sir Robin Butler, after accusing the media of making wild accusations and prejudging the issue, admitting that the prosecution of the Matrix Churchill executives had gone ahead even though an important argument in their defence had been accepted by senior officials in Whitehall.[9]

On 8 November Lady Thatcher herself appeared and led us

to believe that she, the most hands-on Prime Minister in living memory, had been unaware of what was going on. 'If I'd seen every copy of every minute sent in government, I would be in a snowstorm. I could not have done my job as Prime Minister if I had got involved in these things.' She went on to brush aside or ignore many of the questions put to her either by Lord Justice Scott or by his counsel, Presiley Baxendale QC. Asked why the original guidelines, which had been decided in 1984, were not told to Parliament for another eleven months, she replied that this had been a matter for Lord Howe. 'He had great responsibilities and was fully capable of discharging those responsibilities. I fully accepted the Foreign Secretary's judgement.' Had she known about that secret decision in 1988 to revise the guidelines in view of the fact that her private secretary, Sir Charles Powell, had told the Foreign Secretary that 'the Prime Minister wanted to be kept closely in touch with all relevant decisions at every stage'? Lady Thatcher responded that she had never been informed of the new guidelines. The new wording 'did not come to me'.[10]

Reminded that another of her private secretaries had mentioned the guidelines in a document sent to her before a Cabinet meeting in July 1989, she said she had not appreciated its significance. 'I was concerned with the big issue.' The change in the government's approach to Iraq amounted to 'a change in circumstances, not a change in policy'. Later she said she thought it would have been 'better had a summary of the decision come to me'. It must certainly have come as something of surprise to her ex-Ministers that she had been above the mundane business of everyday decision-making: 'Delegation matters in government.'[11]

Commenting on 31 March 1994 on the progress of the inquiry, the *Financial Times* stated that the evidence appeared to prove beyond reasonable doubt that: Britain's arms licensing system was designed to allow the export of potentially lethal equipment; that Ministers and officials breached their own guidelines and that the government kept its guidelines from Parliament for nearly a year, later giving misleading answers; that Ministers and officials approved arms exports to Jordan and Saudi Arabia, ignoring intelligence information that those countries were being used as conduits to send arms to Iraq; that there were serious failings in the way intelligence information was disseminated; that during the Matrix Churchill trial inadequate procedures were followed by government lawyers in general and by Sir Nicholas Lyell in particular, and that documents made available to the inquiry showed that if Ministers never deliberately lied to Parliament, they acted on advice from their officials which covered up policy.

Writing before the outcome of the Scott Inquiry, the best summation of what has gone on comes from Richard Norton-Taylor of the *Guardian*, who has followed the Matrix Churchill affair from its outset: 'Over the past six months, with the help of more than 130,000 documents and with none of the deference of Commons committees, Lord Justice Scott and Presiley Baxendale QC have extracted from witnesses an unprecedented insight into the Whitehall machine, into the relations between civil servants, between departments, between officials and their Ministers. They have unveiled incompetence, arrogance, dissembling, buck-passing. They have shown how Ministers, encouraged by officials, misled Parliament and even, in the words of Mark Higson, a former Foreign Office official, how civil servants "lied to each other". They have unearthed a deep cynicism – a kind of poisoning of the intellect – which is endemic in Whitehall and stretches far beyond the government's policy towards the sale of arms to Saddam Hussein.'[12]

An Opportunist on a Gravy Train –
The Thatcher Connection

On 2 October 1994 the *Observer* ran a front-page story to the effect that Mark Thatcher, the son of the former Prime Minister, was about to be sued under US anti-racketeering laws over allegations that he was party to fraudulent dealings in a Texas aircraft fuel company. William King, a Houston lawyer, says that he will be suing Mark Thatcher for alleged conspiracy to fraud, claiming that he had duped his client, John Laughlin, founder of the firm Ameristar, after it had been taken over by David Wallace,

Chief Executive of the Grantham Company and a former treasurer of the Thatcher Foundation in the USA. Mark Thatcher set up the Grantham Company (named after his mother's birthplace) in partnership with Wallace in the early 1980s. Grantham has invested in various home security companies and specialises in renting security systems to the seriously rich.

The media and some MPs have been chasing after the elusive Mr Thatcher for years, not least because he has amassed a multi-million pound fortune very quickly. Mark Thatcher has consistently refused to discuss the matter. With regard to Mr Laughlin and Ameristar, he denies having had anything to do with the takeover, although, according to reports in both the *Guardian* and *The Sunday Times*[14] (among others) he later moved his office from Dallas to Ameristar's office in Houston. The Houston office is shared by the Thatcher Foundation.

The question of Mark Thatcher's millions (variously estimated at between £20m and £40m) has been interesting not least because he showed no early promise of any great financial wizardry or business acumen, even if he did marry a Texas oil heiress. As *The Sunday Times* has pointed out (9.10.94), that paper alone has spent 'countless hours of the past decade trying to uncover the truth behind one of the great intrigues of the 1980s'. Namely, how did Thatcher do it? After leaving Harrow he went to the accountants Touche Ross, where he failed his accountancy examinations three times. In 1979 he set up Monteagle Marketing, which he described as 'an international consultancy'. It went into voluntary liquidation in 1985. He also tried his hand at male modelling and racing driving. During his brief career as a would-be Nigel Mansell, he hit the headlines when he was ignominiously rescued having lost himself in the desert.

In 1992 he was named in a US court in connection with a $4bn payment made to a Saudi Arabian by Rolls-Royce and British Aerospace for assisting them to do a deal with Saudi Arabia. During the same year allegations were made about him in a book by Ari Ben-Menashe, a former Israeli intelligence officer, that he had been involved in arms deals with the Chilean weapons manufacturer Carlos Cardoen. This latter information was raised in the Commons but never received any satisfactory response.

Mark Thatcher's millions have enabled him to enjoy a lavish lifestyle with expensive homes in Dallas and London's Belgravia, the latter said to have cost £2m. He also had a *pied-à-terre* in Switzerland until fairly recently, when he became involved in a disagreement with the Swiss authorities.

His name has been linked to deals in the Middle East since 1982, when questions were raised over his involvement with the building of a university in Oman by Cementation, a British company owned by Lord Matthews, a close associate of Mrs Thatcher, then Prime Minister. The exact part he played in the deal has never been explained.

Mr Thatcher has not endeared himself to the British media, whatever their political persuasion, by always refusing to answer any questions and consistently being both rude and arrogant.

Then, on 9 October 1994, a week after the racketeering story, *The Sunday Times* ran a front-page story and two inside pages (backed up by tape recordings and transcripts) under the banner headline 'Revealed: Mark Thatcher's Secret Profit from £20-billion Arms Deal'. Mark Thatcher, the paper claims, made his initial fortune back in 1984 by helping fix the biggest arms deal of the century while his mother was Prime Minister. 'He was part of a team of middlemen who earned a secret £240m commission for brokering the Al Yamamah agreement to supply British jet fighters, naval mine-hunters and ammunition to Saudi Arabia,' the report claimed. His cut, it said, was £12m.

Documents, transcripts of bugged conversations and tape recordings held by the paper show, it said, Mark Thatcher's role in the deal. The tape recordings implicating him were made by Saudi intelligence agents monitoring rival bids by Britain, France and the USA, and the transcripts were supplied by Mohammed Khilewi, a Saudi First Secretary at the United Nations. In May Khilewi defected to the USA, where he was granted political asylum after revealing details of his country's nuclear programme. Company sources involved in the deal have confirmed both Thatcher's role and the total amount of commissions involved. The story is long and complex and cannot be given in full here, but it includes the allegation that a senior civil servant, Sir Clive Whitmore, then a Permanent Secretary at the Ministry of Defence and former

Private Secretary to Margaret Thatcher, was sent by worried British officials involved in the negotiations to deliver 'a witch's warning' about the potentially disastrous consequences of her son's involvement, a warning that she ignored. The Ministry of Defence has denied this.

Following rumours and allegations circulating throughout the late 1980s, the House of Commons Public Accounts Committee set up an inquiry whose findings were noted as long ago as 1991. After the committee's Chairman, Sir Robert Sheldon, took advice from the Ministry of Defence, it was decided that no report could be published. There has been speculation ever since that while it is possible that nothing illegal was uncovered, there was reference to commissions. At the time of writing (autumn 1994) attempts are being made to force the report's publication. Shadow Trade and Industry Secretary Robin Cook, speaking before the 1994 Conservative Party Conference, said, 'There are two main questions that must be answered: what influence did Mark Thatcher sell in return for his millions, and how much did Margaret Thatcher use her public office to promote her son to make a private fortune? She now stands accused of letting her son use her public position to feather his nest with the biggest hand-out on record.'

This is not a good time for Thatcher junior. As well as the case now being brought against him by Mr Laughlan in the States, and the allegations regarding the Saudi arms deal, he has also been mentioned in connection with the Scott Inquiry and the Pergan Dam affair.

All those now looking into Mark Thatcher's various activities in general, and the 1984 Saudi deal in particular, agree that it is unlikely that what he did, whatever it was, and the part he played, whatever *that* was, will prove improper. What is in question is how he was allowed to profit from his mother being Prime Minister and why she did nothing to stop it. The 1919 Whitehall protocol, *Questions of Procedure for Ministers*, states that 'Ministers will want to see that no conflict arises nor appears to arise between their private interests and their public duties'. It does not say, 'except in the case of the Prime Minister'.

As to Mark himself, a former British Aerospace executive involved in the 1984 Saudi negotiations put it like this: 'Mark

Thatcher was an opportunist on a gravy train, scooping whatever money he could from these deals. He touted his name and position in relation to Margaret Thatcher and became a name on the lips of everyone trying to secure business with the Saudi royals.'

Chapter 12

CLEANING OUT THE STY

'. . . a certain class of dishonesty, dishonesty magnificent in its proportions, and climbing into high places, has become at the same time so rampant and so splendid that there seems to be reason for fearing that men and women will be taught to feel that dishonesty if it can become splendid, will cease to be abominable. If dishonesty can live in a gorgeous palace with pictures on all its walls, and gems in all its cupboards, with marble and ivory in all its corners, and can give Apician dinners, and get into Parliament, and deal in millions, then dishonesty is not disgraceful, and the man dishonest after such a fashion is not a low scoundrel.'
  Anthony Trollope, *An Autobiography,* 1883

Trollope was writing towards the end of an extensive period of parliamentary, political and social reform. Those who, like many of us, tended to slumber through history lessons on nineteenth-century legislation now need, in view of what has happened during the last fifteen years, to rediscover just why such wide-sweeping reforms of public life had become necessary: reforms brought about in spite of the opposition of those fighting to maintain the status quo. The First Reform Act of 1832 was drawn up when the country was still riddled with rotten boroughs and only a relatively small proportion of the male population was allowed to vote, those votes having to be cast in public since there was no such thing as a secret ballot. Nor was there any check on electoral bribery and corruption. Patronage was rife in the country's administration, including especially entry into the civil service. There was no obligation on anyone to provide decent housing, clean water or even sewerage. It took the massive epidemics of diseases such as cholera and typhoid, which peaked in 1849 when the stink of the Thames actually permeated the Houses of Parliament, to improve the provision of the latter.

The First Reform Act did at least do away with a proportion of the rotten boroughs (some 143 of them) and enlarged the number of those entitled to vote, enfranchising male householders in the towns and cities who owned property with a rateable value of £10 or more. Social legislation followed shortly after, banning such things as women and small children working underground in mines and limiting the length of the working day which, in 1844, could be as much as sixteen hours. British industry immediately announced that this would lead to destitution and the ruination of the nation's economy. *Plus ça change. . . .*

In 1853 the Act was introduced which ended patronage in the civil service and, in the words of Sir Stafford Northcote and Sir Charles Trevelyan, who had been asked to report on the matter, 'the employment of the indolent and incapable . . . and those whose abilities do not warrant success in this field'. Entry was to be by competitive public examination with a view to ensuring that from then on the civil service would be neutral and not biased towards any one political party.

In 1854 the Corrupt Practices Prevention Act was brought in. Under its provisions, parliamentary candidates could be punished for using threats, bribery, coercion, personation and 'treating' to get elected.

The Second Reform Act in 1867 redistributed the majority of parliamentary seats: up to that time Cornwall, for instance, had returned as many MPs as Middlesex and all the London boroughs north of the Thames. In spite of the earlier Act, about half the population were still represented by just thirty-four MPs, while the other half returned 380. The Act also enfranchised a further swathe of people including not only those who owned property but also those who lodged in it or paid rent towards its rateable value. The secret ballot was introduced in 1872.

1874 and 1875 saw two further pieces of social reform. Local authorities were given new powers to abolish slums and build new homes for rent under the Artisans' and Labourers' Dwellings Improvements Act, and the working week was cut again to between fifty and sixty hours. The 1875 Public Health Act appointed Medical Officers of Health to monitor and deal with health problems, provoking the *Economist* to warn that 'suffering and evil are nature's admonitions – the impatient attempts of benevolence to banish them have always been more productive of evil than good'.

In 1883, the year Trollope's autobiography was published, a further Corrupt and Illegal Practices Bill went through Parliament, defining the role of party agents and limiting the amount that could be spent on election expenses, those expenses to be the responsibility of duly appointed agents and properly accounted for. In the same year the Cheap Transport Act made it obligatory for all the railway companies to offer cheap workmen's fares. A Third Reform Act widened the male franchise still further, enabling those living in rural communities to vote for the first time, and the 1885 Redistribution Act brought about further comprehensive boundary changes. In 1888 the Local Government Act established sixty-two new *elected* County Councils, elections to take place every three years.

Listing the above is salutary for, as Chris Painter, a senior lecturer at the University of Central England Business School writes in the July–September 1994 issue of the *Political Quarterly*,[1] 'The democratic system established in the late nineteenth century is progressively being dismantled, whole swathes of local administration handed over to Whitehall appointees. The debate is now centred on the potential abuse of a system of hand-picked appointees and the opportunities of any governing party to pack them with politically sympathetic nominees. The very composition of these bodies can thus become an effective means of mobilising bias, ever-enlarging the party patronage system.' It is also as well to point out here that the great nineteenth-century reforms did not come about because of the naturally enlightened outlook of the governments of the day. From the Chartists onwards it took everything from public petitions to riots and bloodshed to achieve reform, bringing down a substantial number of governments in the process.

*   *   *

CLEANING OUT THE STY

The obvious question the current catalogue of sleaze raises is: what can be done about it? While it may well be, as Hugo Young is quoted earlier as saying, that privately many senior Conservatives are worried about the party being seen as representing the sleaze constituency, it does not appear that any plans are in hand to alter the situation. Quangos, placemen and jobs for the boys and girls are still defended as improving efficiency, providing decentralisation, giving people more choice, etc, etc. Indeed, on the BBC's *Today* programme on 17 October 1994, government spokesman David Hunt stoutly defended the government's record, claiming that it has cut back Quangos by a third or more. When his interviewer, James Naughtie, exploded at this assertion, Hunt added defensively that he (Naughtie) was including the various executive bodies and agencies, hospital trusts, etc, and that these were not truly Quangos. He added that these bodies were now 'more accountable' to local people, without explaining how this could be.

Nor has the present administration any interest in a Bill of Rights; it obviously considers that it has gone far enough in implementing a Freedom of Information Act. Parliamentary reform is not on the cards, while sheer political survival ensures that political funding will remain secret and unaccountable. The Rivers will continue to flow. Faced with the greed of directors and Chief Executives with their telephone number salaries and crazy rolling contracts, which renew themselves afresh every morning, Ministers merely mumble about self-regulation while exhorting the rest of the work force to tighten their belts and be content with pay rises of 2.5 per cent or less, telling them the while that there is no such thing as a job for life any more.

To quote Chris Painter again, the excuse used for doing away with public accountability and the transfer of power and huge sums of money to undemocratic bodies is that what really matters is the quality of the services and the means of making them responsive rather than the need for them to be democratically elected. 'There is now,' he writes, 'no way of legally enforcing standards and there are few rights of access to information.' There is a desperate need for research into how nomination and selection procedures work.

First Quangos and patronage. The best the government seems prepared to offer, while defending the present system, is to 'look into' how appointments are made. At the time of writing Labour has not produced a policy document, but Tony Blair, when raising the latest cash-for-questions scandal on 21 October 1994, called for the immediate publication of the names, remuneration, perks and political allegiance of all those sitting on Quangos. He also stated that there should be a ban on Ministers leaving government and immediately taking up remunerative posts on the boards of the industries they themselves had privatised. The Liberal Democrats addressed Quangos in some detail at their 1994 Conference, although this passed unnoticed in a welter of media coverage on votes about cannabis and the monarchy.

Yet it is a subject which now concerns a substantial number of people of varying interests and across the party political divides: how do we replace the existing system with one which is both democratic and accountable? Peter Hennessy, Professor of Contemporary History at Queen Mary and Westfield College, London, considers that it will be necessary to begin at once to rebuild the arteries and conduits of democracy throughout the nation.[2] Elections empower the community; nominations entrench authority. The worst of all worlds would be the replacement of one oligarchy by another of a different political colour, something which might prove all too tempting with the system so firmly entrenched.

Professor Hennessy also noted in his inaugural lecture to the college how flimsy were the safeguards to our constitution, a constitution which he described as the 'Great Ghost', so difficult is it to track down its detail.[3] 'If I were a Cabinet Minister,' he said, 'I would worry about the meagreness of my procedural defences against the risk of an overmighty premiership. And such matters belong not just to the party forming the government-of-the-day, but to all democratically elected aspirants to a place at the Cabinet table. . . .'

So what can be done about the countless Quangos and agencies? At least a start might be made by considering the proposals offered first by the Liberal Democrats and then by Democratic Audit.[4]

Liberal Democrats

Their policy statement sets out the present position and calls for both a reduction in the number of Quangos and the transfer of their power, wherever practicable, to democratic institutions. It also calls for:

- an effective means by which local government and Parliament can scrutinise the work of remaining Quangos and hold them to account for their use of public funds, including making Quangos subject to the same rules as local authorities for publicising their business, registering interests and holding their meetings in public.
- the replacement, where practicable, of ministerial appointees with local Councillors or representatives appointed by relevent Parliamentary Select Committees or local authorities.
- at a European level, increased scrutiny of the Commission and other unelected European bodies by the European Parliament.
- a review of all existing appointments of Chairs to Quangos immediately on coming to power.
- a full-scale 'Quango audit' with a view to disbanding unnecessary bodies and transferring their responsibilities to others.
- an open public register to be kept, giving details of the membership and remit of all Quangos and similar bodies, including the names, duties, responsibilities and expenses of executive and non-executive appointments, as well as membership of, or donations to, political parties over the previous five years.
- an immediate review of the performance of the existing senior executive members of Quangos undertaken by an independent review body.
- all appointments to remaining Quangos to be made in accordance with good equal opportunities practice and with a view to ensuring balanced representation of all parts of the community.

The Lib-Dems further state that District and Regional Health Authorities should be incorporated into democratically elected local authorities, that grant-maintained schools and colleges should be brought back within the framework of local strategic planning, that there should be provision for all housing association committees to include in their membership a proportion of elected Councillors, and that all the Home Secretary's appointees should be removed from the new police authorities in England and Wales and local authority representation restored to two-thirds of their total membership.

Democratic Audit

This body calls for:

- a review of which non-elected bodies should properly become elected bodies; of the opportunities to introduce 'user' representation on to local public bodies; and of the variety of possible relationships such bodies might have with local government.
- a recasting of the categories into which all public bodies are placed, taking into account the requirement of openness, consultation, scrutiny and accountability which might be appropriate for each category of public bodies, and recognising also the need of certain types of body (academic, cultural, etc) for independence from government and shorter-term political accountability.
- the re-introduction of a statutory 'right to know', incorporating best practice from Freedom of Information laws in other mature democracies, the prohibition of 'gagging' contracts and a code for whistle-blowers.
- new provisions in public law, including new statutory machinery on the Australian or US model, to ensure that all public bodies, including departmental executive agencies, meet basic standards of consultation, open decision-making and equitable conduct.
- a review of ministerial patronage and measures to ensure a proper degree of pluralism in public appointments and to subject patronage powers to democratic openness and accountability.

*   *   *

Side by side with such a far-reaching overhaul, there will need to be drastic political reforms to bring Parliament into the twentieth century, let alone the twenty-first. On the crucial question of electoral reform, only the Liberal Democrats express whole-hearted support for a system of proportional representation, although there is now a growing body of opinion in the Labour Party which also sees it as inevitable. However, in *A New Constitution for Britain* by Tony Benn and Andrew Hood, published in 1994,[5] Mr Benn, representing the traditional Labour view, dismisses the very notion of PR in a few sentences. Up until now the first-past-the-post system has been nicely predictable in that it ensures a parliamentary majority accountable only through fear of losing that majority at the next general election. That fear gone, as one of the book's reviewers points out,[6] all accountability is eroded. Yet for Mr Benn nothing is wrong with the existing system except the failure of an effective Opposition.

Andrew Hood, on the other hand, argues that with a shift to a three or three-and-a-half party system, first-past-the-post can no longer deliver accountable government, since one party can govern indefinitely with only 40 per cent of the vote, while mid-term protest leads only to rearrangements within the ruling party. 'Democratic politics then become purely internal to the ruling party and its supporters, with everyone else as the audience' – which is where we came in with Tom Paine's quote at the beginning of this book. Mr Hood continues, 'The erosion of social and economic rights has taken place at the hands of administrations which have depended for their electoral support on the grossly inequitable distribution of the popular vote south east of a line from Severn to Wash, where 52 per cent of the vote delivers 92 per cent of the seats.'

Then there are obvious administrative reforms which could be made to the conduct of parliamentary business, such as the hours the House of Commons sits (a throw-back to the days before the Reform Acts) and the number of weeks it is in session, however much business there might be or whatever the current national or international situation. But even to begin to attract respect, the process needs to go further than administrative reform and the doing away with ludicrous procedures such as MPs on occasion passing folding opera hats around the Chamber to enable them to speak and the farce which is now Prime Minister's Question Time. What price efficiency, leaner-and-fitter practices, value for money and improved productivity in today's House of Commons?

One way of improving parliamentary and government accountability would be to strengthen the role of the parliamentary Select Committees. Even now they can be a force, as has been shown by the sterling work of the Public Accounts Committees. It is widely canvassed that committees should carry out more systematic examinations of proposed legislation by taking evidence and reporting on White Papers and other consultative documents.[7] Specialised committees should look at Bills immediately after their presentation to Parliament, thus avoiding the kind of badly drafted, ad hoc legislation typified by the recent Criminal Justice Bill. They could also take evidence at the committee stages of Bills. Departmentally related committees might also then review the operation of all important Acts two or three years after they have come into force, thus playing a more positive role in the scrutiny of legislation throughout the entire process.

It would then behove government to take notice of what the committees reported back to Parliament, rather than choosing to ignore most of their recommendations as at present. As it is, the existing system of Select Committees does not possess effective means of calling Ministers to account for their policies and actions – policies and actions which they currently shrug off on the grounds that they are no longer responsible for what happens, that responsibility having been passed on to the relevent Quango or executive agency. The need to strengthen the power of the committees requires that pressure be put on MPs not only by political commentators and those patronisingly referred to as 'the chattering classes', but by the media and, most of all, by the public who are at the receiving end of what government decides. The stronger and reorganised committees could then be put to use in the legislative field. These ideas have come from, among others, the Hansard Society Commission in its paper published in 1994, *Making the Law*. As it is, 'democracy' now largely consists of shuffling up to the polling booth and making a cross once every four or five years. No wonder so many people no longer bother to vote.

Even those MPs who take their jobs seriously find themselves without a voice. The Select Committee on Procedure is currently studying a recommendation for sweeping reforms to restore to backbench MPs an evens chance of piloting legislation on to the statute book; this in the wake of the shambles over the proposed Civil Rights (Disabled Persons) Bill. In his evidence to the committee, Labour MP Alf Morris, who was Minister for the Disabled in the last Labour administration, recommended that the top seven Bills in the private members' ballot be guaranteed time to complete their scrutiny if it is demonstrated that they command the support of a majority of MPs. This would prevent such Bills being killed off for lack of time by a minority of MPs of any party acting on the orders of the party whips. Morris claimed that private members were rapidly losing to the executive all power to change the law by means of such Bills.

Accusing the government of dishonesty, he said, 'If the executive gives the impression that a Bill will have a fair run and that they want to see it improved in committee – only to wreck the Bill by unloading scores of amendments at the report stage – they stand guilty of being less than frank with Parliament and the electorate.' He cited the example of the belated amendments to the Disabled Persons Bill detailed earlier. Unless debates on Private Members' Bills with majority support are properly timetabled, Mr Morris continued, everyone is wasting their time. The Select Committee has yet to report on the matter.

Other much-needed reforms include details of, and limits to, political funding. This would deal with the amount above which details of a donation should be publicly acknowledged. As we have seen, the consensus would seem to be about £5,000. At the same time there should be discussion as to whether or not donations are acceptable from non-British nationals who do not vote here and may well not even live in the UK.

The Register of Members' Interests should be made truly statutory and provide details of exactly how much each Member is paid by whom and for what, alongside a Register of Lobby Groups. This alone would require a major overhaul of current practice, but it is not an impossible task by any stretch of the imagination.

From the point of view of citizens, a large number of whom still continue to stand, in Tom Paine's words, 'torpidly by', we need a true Bill of Rights and a proper Freedom of Information Act. With regard to the latter it is remarkable, as I mentioned in a previous book calling for just such an Act,[8] that many of those who shout loudest about doing away with the 'nanny' state telling us what to do appear to be only too happy for 'nanny to know best' when it comes to what we should routinely be told and what should be kept from us. Neither a Bill of Rights nor a Freedom of Information Act can be considered to be in the remotest way radical: virtually every other civilised nation has had both for years. A Freedom of Information Act would shine a light into all those dark corners and illuminate all those shady goings-on which lead, among many other things, to the misuse of patronage and the treating of the country by any political party as if it were a private fiefdom.

Both the Labour Party and Liberal Democrats have in the past promised a Bill of Rights and a Freedom of Information Act, though we have yet to learn exactly what Labour's new leader, Tony Blair, has to say on the subject. The temptation for an in-coming Labour government must be merely to tinker with the system, not change it. This is simply not good enough.

The country is fed up with sleaze. Young people are turned off political involvement in droves, to the point where they do not even bother to vote. They are endlessly exhorted to do as I say, not do as I do. The examples provided for them are of a whole layer of people who are doing very nicely thank you out of the Sleaze System: the businessmen with huge salaries, rolling contracts, massive share options and delicious perks, no matter how inefficient and disastrous they might be; placemen getting nice little earners in Quangos for a couple of days' work a week; and politicians who thunder on about family values and single parents, while impregnating their mistresses and running two households; politicians who hymn the virtues of salary restraint and the abolition of the minimum wage, while accepting thousands of pounds in extra-curricular activities outside their parliamentary duties and who are even prepared to take payment for asking questions in the House of Commons to which they have been sent – lest they forget – by ordinary voters.

It is time to clean out the sty.

POSTSCRIPT

A round-up at the end of January 1995 shows that while there have been no more scandals over cash-for-questions or amorous MPs, everything else is going on exactly as before. The good news is that the Nolan Committee is now sitting and that within three days of its commencement Lord Nolan was already implying that he was likely to recommend real curbs on MPs' privileges. His suggestions included doing away with self-regulation and bringing in outside regulators, stricter and mandatory disclosure of interests and a ban on the taking of fees from commercial lobbyists.

This led to the immediate appearance on newscasts of a string of Conservative backbenchers intoning that Parliament was a sovereign body and that they did not want 'outsiders' coming in to regulate them, thank you very much. At the outset, Lord Nolan had been told by, among others, Labour's Roy Hattersley, that there was a suspicion in the country that the committee had been set up merely to quell disquiet and that nothing was likely to come of it. Ivor Crewe, Professor of Politics at Essex University, spoke of a nation which regarded its politicians as self-serving hypocrites who put party before country and self before party, while Lord Blake, a Tory peer, said Britain was living in the most corrupt era since Edwardian times and blamed the government's being too long in office: 'MPs should not just reveal the jobs they do in the Register of Members' Interests, but also the amount of money they receive.'

On the second day of Lord Nolan's inquiry, Dame Angela Rumbold, a former Tory Minister, admitted to receiving a salary of £12,000 from a commercial lobbyist, but claimed that she had never asked a question for her paymasters. She had resigned as a director of the company concerned, Decision Makers, in October 1994 following allegations (which she denied) that she had used her influence to persuade the government to choose a particular station as a crucial link on the line to the Channel Tunnel on behalf of clients of the firm. At that time she had been a Deputy Party Chairman. Correspondence from Decision Makers to Blue Circle, read out before the committee, stated that Dame Angela had been 'able to keep the party fully appraised of Blue Circle's plans in the East Thames corridor'.

The *Observer*'s front-page story on 22 January 1995 revealed that Ministers and MPs were employing political lobbyists in the guise of 'political researchers'. Quoting the *Register of Interests of Members' Secretaries and Research Assistants,* it noted that eighteen people working for the aforesaid MPs and Ministers declared a 'relevant gainful occupation' with lobbyists, public affairs and political consultancies. Another ten were working as in-house consultants with companies which included British Aerospace, British Petroleum and GEC Marconi. This particular register, unlike that of members' interests, is not for public scrutiny but is restricted to those with access to the Commons library. One of the most high-profile interests declared is that of Dame Angela's researcher and former constituency agent, Oliver Colvile, who had worked for Decision Makers at the same time as he was working for her as a Commons researcher.

Asked about Mr Colvile, Dame Angela denied that there had ever been any connection with the lobby company: 'Of course there would have been a conflict of interest had it ever arisen, but the question never arose. If you print that, then don't blame me if you have a problem. That's just not true.' She was, she continued, absolutely fed up with people trying to blacken her name. When she was informed that Mr Colvile had registered his interest with Decision Makers, Dame Angela responded, 'I am gobsmacked . . . I had no idea he could be working for any other interest.' The relevation, she continued, rendered her 'speechless'.

The register also shows that Chris Mockler, a consultant to Market Access International, whose clients include the drug company Merck Sharp Dohme, was employed as a researcher in 1994 by Marion Roe, Tory Chairman of the Commons' Health Committee. Other researchers with potentially conflicting outside interests worked for Foreign Office Minister Tony Baldry, Environment Minister Sir Paul Beresford and Social Security Minister Alistair Burt.

The Nolan Committee is expected to publish its recommendations at the end of May 1995.

Westminster Council

The investigation into the dealings of Westminster Council did not recommence until well into January 1993, not least because Dame Shirley Porter was still abroad. On 13 January 1995 Frank Dobson, now Labour's Shadow Environment Spokesman, and Peter Bradley, leader of the Council's Labour Group, held a joint press conference to mark the anniversary of the Magill Interim Report.

They complained of government inaction over the provisional findings in the report and of the Audit Commission's failure to provide adequate resources to tackle the 'incompetence' of the Council. Fourteen new objections have been submitted to the auditor and a further five are pending. Together they represent an alleged improper expenditure of £100m.

Bradley claimed that Westminster's finances were now teetering 'on the edge of complete breakdown and senior management is simply not able to cope as crisis follows crisis'. He said it was almost impossible to overstate the depth and breadth of the gerrymandering and that almost every function of the Council – from deporting the homeless to targeting new parking spaces in marginal wards – was turned to use by the Conservative majority. It was now five and a half years since the first objection was made and, at the current rate of progress, it would take well into the twenty-first century before Mr Gummer stopped saying the matter was *sub judice*. The Council was still being run by politicians and officials in key posts who were deeply implicated in the affair. Frank Dobson is now calling on the National Audit Office to investigate the government's 1990 rate support grant settlement which enabled Westminster to set its poll tax at £195 in the run-up to that year's local elections.

On 7 February 1995 Anthony Scrivener, QC made a statement in defence of Dame Shirley Porter on the last day of the Inquiry into Westminster's housing policy. He stated that the council house sales policy was 'a lawful means of implementing government policy regarding home ownership, not a means of boosting Conservative votes.' All the designated sales could be justified on housing and planning grounds. Of 4,782 designated sales, only 339 were in marginally political wards. Mr Scrivener said that the district auditor, John Magill, had been given the wrong legal advice, that his methodology was unorthodox and that there was 'no evidence to support the conclusion that Dame Shirley had a wicked motive'.

'The Council was never found to have been in breach of its statutory duty to the homeless. The Council houses 1,915 families which is more than most other London Boroughs.' Mr Scrivener also told the Inquiry that it represented 'the most expensive audit process ever in the history of auditing in the UK'.

The Inquiry is expected to report in the summer of 1995. Meanwhile, Mr Magill will have to decide whether or not his findings on gerrymandering, spelled out in his interim report, remain valid. If he decides they are, then he can either issue surcharge notices under the Local Government Finance Act of 1982 or he can apply to the High Court for payment; the latter could be contested. After hearing Mr Scrivener's statement, a spokesman for the Council's Conservative group said: 'At least the other side of the argument has been heard. We believe nobody did anything wrong at all. They took legal advice and acted on it to the letter.'

Quangos

In spite of widespread criticism across the political spectrum, Quangos are still being set up, while those in existence continue to go strong. Lord Nolan has received many requests to look into who sits on them and how such people are chosen. Simon Jenkins, former editor of *The Times*, called for an independent commission to oversee such appointments; he spoke of the 'packing' of Quangos with the wives of Tory MPs and how members were picked after telephone requests to find someone 'sound' or someone 'sauntering' up to a likely candidate at a party and asking if he or she would like the job.

On 15 January the *Observer* carried a story stating that strong evidence of the sleaze and bungling of government Quangos had been slipped into the House of Commons library by Welsh Secretary John Redwood, following a £175,000 investigation by civil servants and a firm of City accountants. Mr Redwood has rejected calls to publish the report in full. It was yet another inquiry into the performance of Welsh Quangos and identified weaknesses of personnel and payroll matters, petty cash controls and purchasing policies. It proposed 'a wide range of single signatory limits and signing practices' for Quango cheques and explained that some members did not 'understand the reason for commercially run bank accounts'. Other clean-up proposals suggested that there was proof of gifts and hospitality to Quango members. Three days later reports in the press noted that our old friends the Ministry of Defence had wasted hundreds of thousands of pounds on appointing staff to a new Quango which almost immediately had to be wound up.

The Ministry had signed six-figure contracts with senior staff to run the now defunct Housing Trust, which was to take over the management of service housing. The scheme collapsed after the Treasury would not offer the City backers a guaranteed rate of return on their investment in the huge housing estates. The Chief Executive designate, Mike Robinson, would have received £240,000 plus option bonuses totalling £60,000. Other senior staff were to have received equally huge salaries, way above those paid for equivalent jobs in local government, where housing officers earn on average £15,000 a year.

It has also been revealed that Ron Harrison, the Chief Executive of the Student Loan Company (which, as has been noted previously, is currently under investigation for alleged corruption and mismanagement), has been reappointed for a further three years on a £250,000 contract, a fact which came to light in a parliamentary answer to Labour MP Stephen Byers. Harrison had been expected to go at the end of January 1995, but he was apparently given the extended contract in an unpublicised deal in 1994. The company is currently undergoing what is described as 'a forensic audit' by the National Audit Office, following fresh corruption allegations. Mr Harrison is on indefinite sick leave.

The Trough

Meanwhile, the sound of snouts chomping in the trough has become deafening. There has been the mega 75 per cent rise awarded to British Gas Chief Executive Cedric Brown, bringing his salary up to £450,000 at a time when ordinary employees are being asked to take pay cuts and the company is cutting back on its safety checks by 90 per cent! Several other British Gas executives received increases of between 32 and 50 per cent.

James Smith, Chairman of Eastern Electricity, had his salary raised by £33,000 to £250,000 in spite of his decision to work only a three-day week. On paper his pay has been cut to £105,000, but Eastern Electricity had to admit that he was also drawing a substantial pension – in the region of £140,000 a year – which he was 'perfectly entitled to'. Over at Midland, Mr Smith's opposite number, Bryan Townsend, is paid £290,000 per year for a two-day week, part of which is a pension.

The chairmen of the ten privatised water companies have received salary rises of up to 571 per cent and shared in multi-million pound share and pension packages. Twenty-five senior water company directors have become at least £500,000 better off since privatisation, including five who have become millionaires.

The NHS

Charge and counter-charge as to the state of the NHS continue to ring through the airwaves. On 20 January 1995 Jeremy Lee-Potter, ex-Chairman of the BMA, a Tory voter and the man who did all he could to reconcile the NHS professionals to the changes, announced he was taking early retirement, accusing the government of sacrificing the NHS to narrow political dogma and allowing no real debate. After going into considerable detail as to just what was happening, he said, 'I think it is quite wrong for trust boards to be packed with the wives of Tory MPs, members of the local Conservative Party, industrialists who contribute to party funds. They should be open to everyone, who would then be vetted by an independent elected body.' His conclusion was, 'I get the feeling that we are facing a situation not dissimilar to when Douglas-Home lost the election. In those days it was Rachmanism. There was a general stench that was arising from the government which everyone could smell.'

General

On 15 January 1995 the *Independent on Sunday* noted that the takeover battle for Northern Electricity by Trafalgar House 'was hotting up'. Trafalgar House is 26 per cent owned by an associate company of Jardine Matheson, Hongkong Land, which has been one of the largest contributors to the Conservative Party. Since 1979 Trafalgar House itself has donated £600,000 to party funds. It was also revealed that Tessa Keswick, wife of Jardine Matheson executive Henry Keswick, works for the Chancellor, Kenneth Clarke, and has done so since 1989, when he was at the Department of Health. Trafalgar House is still waiting to hear from President of the Board of Trade Michael Heseltine whether or not he intends to refer the bid to the Monopolies and Mergers Commission. He has now refused to do so.

POSTSCRIPT

At the time of writing the findings of the Scott Inquiry are still awaited.

A timely reminder that no party when in government has been immune from sleaze was the death during the first week of the Nolan Inquiry of convicted fraudster Lord Kagan, otherwise known as 'Mr Gannex'. He was ennobled by, and a friend of, the then Labour Prime Minister, Harold Wilson.

NOTES

Chapter 1

1. *Hansard* 26.7.77.
2. *EGO Trip* Democratic Audit. ed. S. Weir and W. Hall. Charter 88 and University of Essex. 1994. p.20
3. Ibid.
4. *Observer* 3.7.94
5. Ibid.
6. *Guardian* 15.4.94.
7. Ibid.
8. *Health and Social Services Journal* 12.11.92, 'Secretary Resigns Amid Patronage Abuse Row', and 26.11.94, 'Keeping up with the Joneses'.
9. *47th Report of the Committee of Public Accounts. The Welsh Development Agency Accounts 1991–92.* HMSO 16.6.93.
10. Annual Register of Events, 1954.

Chapter 2

1. *EGO Trip* Democratic Audit.
2. *Times* 8.7.94; *Guardian* 8.7.94.
3. *Hansard* 8.7.94.
4. *Guardian* 21.4.94 and following.
5. *Guardian* 24.5.94, 25.5.94, 26.5.94.
6. *Hansard* 25.5.94.
7. Written reply by John Major to Archie Kirkwood 22.7.93.
8. *Hansard* 6.12.93
9. Ibid.

Chapter 3

1. *Minority Report of the Home Affairs Committee on the Funding of Political Parties 1993–94*. HMSO 16.3.94.
2. Ibid paragraphs 18–26.
3. 'Covert Company Donations Sent to Tories' and 'The Circuitous Route of Secret Tory Funds'. Both major features, by Rosie Waterhouse and John Piennar, appeared in the *Independent* on 16.1.89.
4. *Minority Report*, paragraph 32.
5. Ibid.
6. Ibid.
7. Copies of letters in reply to Mr Dobson's questions in the possession of the author.
8. *Minority Report*, paragraph 47.

Chapter 4

1. *Birmingham Post* 22.7.91.
2. Ibid. 17.8.91.
3. Ibid.
4. Ibid. 1.9.92.
5. Ibid 11.9.92.
6. *Hansard* 29.10.92.
7. *Post* 26.11.92; *Independent* 27.11.92.
8. *Committee of Public Accounts Report. Wessex Regional Health Authority: Regional Information Systems Plan* 3.11.93.
9. *Health Services Journal* 10.6.93.
10. *Guardian* 15.4.94.
11. Ibid 27.5.94.
12. *Health Services Journal* 26.11.92.

Chapter 5

1. The material in this chapter comes from four sources: personal investigation by the author; documentary information held in the offices of *Voice; Spotlight South West*, BBC local television reports throughout May and June 1992; and *Newsnight*.

Chapter 6

1. *Public Accounts Committee 31st Report. Department of Transport: – The First Sales of Trust Ports*. 27.6.94 and all following in this section.

2. *Guardian* 24.5.94.
3. Ibid.
4. Channel 4 *News at Seven* 26.5.94.
5. *Guardian* 27.5.94.
6. Ibid.
7. *Ministry of Defence Management of the Trident Works Programme.* Report by the Comptroller and Auditor General. July 1994.
8. *Hansard* 26.10.93.
9. *Public Accounts Committee 28th Report. Ministry of Defence: Irregular Expenditure.* 15.3.93.
10. *Hansard* 28.10.92.
11. Parliamentary answers to questions put by Alan Milburn MP, quoted, with table, in *Guardian* 27.4.94.
12. *Independent* and *Guardian* 21.4.94.
13. *Independent* 21.4.94.
14. *Guardian* 21.4.94.
15. *Guardian* 27.5.94.

Chapter 7

1. *Observer* 31.8.94.
2. *For Richer, For Poorer* Alissa Goodman and Steven Webb. Institute for Fiscal Studies, June 1994. *Winners and Losers* Department of Economics, Swansea University. June 1994.
3. *Guardian* 30.5.94.
4. 'Treasury Blocked Rail Deal'. *Guardian* 16.6.94.
5. *Directors' Pay* Labour Research. July 1994.
6. 'Musical Magnate on £9m a Year'. Labour Research. October 1993.
7. Labour Research. October 1993.
8. Labour Research. March 1994.
9. Labour Research. September 1993.
10. Figures given to author from companies' annual reports.
11. *An Accident Waiting to Happen* Judith Cook. Unwin and Hyman. London 1989; *Report of an Inquiry into an Incident at the Lowermoor Water Treatment Works of the SWWA on 6 July 1988* Dr John Lawrence.
12. *Western Morning News* 27.5.94.
13. Ibid. and BBC TV *Spotlight South West* 17.5.94.
14. Figures given to author from companies' annual reports.
15. *Expenditure on the NHS during the Thatcher Years.* Centre for Health Economics, York University. December 1992; *IDS Management Pay Review.* December 1992.
16. *Observer* 7.8.94.

Chapter 8

1. *Blowing the Whistle on Fraud and Corruption* Public Concern at Work. April 1994. The sources of the material on Lambeth are given in the text. The section on Westminster is in part derived from the edition of BBC TV's *Panorama* entitled 'Rotten to the Core'.
2. Quoted in *Observer* 1.5.94.
3. *A Bit on the Side* Paul Halloran and Mark Hollingsworth. Simon and Schuster. 1994.

Chapter 9

1. Figures from Labour Research.
2. Ibid.
3. Halloran and Hollingsworth. op. cit.
4. Ibid. And following.

Chapter 10

1. *Hansard* 18.1.93.
2. Ibid.
3. *Guardian* 19.1.93.
4. *Sunday Telegraph* 9.1.94.
5. Ibid.
6. Ibid.
7. Press release 3.1.94.
8. *Times* 8.7.94.
9. *Financial Times, Guardian* 29.8.94.
10. Ibid.
11. *Guardian* and *Times* 29.8.94.
12. Robin Cook, 'Lord Archer's Story Needs a Final Chapter'. *Guardian* 22.8.94. Also interviewed on BBC Radio 4 *Today*.

Chapter 11

1. *Hansard* 10.5.94.
2. Ibid.
3. *Hansard* 19.5.94.
4. *Hansard* 15.6.94.
5. On 12.5.94 the *Guardian* ran an almost complete transcript of the programme under the heading 'Tory Ministers and MPs are Named in Lobby Scandal'.
6. David Hencke, *Guardian* 9.12.93.

NOTES

7. This and subsequent information in the possession of Mr Byers.
8. *Guardian* 12.9.94.
9. All relevant transcript material in *Guardian* library.
10. *Guardian* and *Independent* 9.12.93.
11. Ibid.
12. *Guardian* 7.12.93.
13. *Sunday Times* 9.10.94; *Guardian* 10.10.94 and others.

Chapter 12

1. 'Restructuring Government', *Political Quarterly* July–September 1994. Volume 65, No. 3.
2. Conversation with author.
3. 'Searching for the Great Ghost: The Palace, the Premiership, the Cabinet and the Constitution in the Post War Period'. February 1994.
4. *EGO Trip* Democratic Audit.
5. Published by Hutchinson.
6. 'Public Service Reform – Reinventing Government'. *Political Quarterly* as above.
7. 'Power on the Back Benches? The Growth of Select Committee Influence.' Derek Hawes, School of Advanced Urban Studies. University of Bristol. 1994.
8. *The Price of Freedom* Hodder & Stoughton 1985; updated NEL 1986.

SELECT BIBLIOGRAPHY

House of Commons Reports

The Implementation and Development of the Technical and Vocational Initiative. Committee of Public Accounts. 10.6.92.

Ministry of Defence: Irregular Expenditure Under an Efficiency Incentive Scheme. Committee of Public Accounts. 15.3.93.

Welsh Development Agency Accounts 1991–92. Committee of Public Accounts. 16.6.93.

West Midlands Regional Health Authority: Regionally Managed Services Organisations. Committee of Public Accounts. 27.10.93.

Wessex Regional Health Authority: Regional Information Systems Plan. Committee of Public Accounts. 3.1.93.

The Proper Conduct of Public Business. Committee of Public Accounts. 17.1.94.

Funding of Political Parties. Home Affairs Committee. 16.3.94.

Department of Transport: The First Sales of Trust Ports. Committee of Public Accounts. 27.6.94.

Quangos and Non-Departmental Public Bodies. House of Commons Library. Research Paper 94/67. 6.5.94.

General Papers and Reports

EGO Trip edited by Stuart Weir and Wendy Hall. Democratic Audit. 1994.

Labour Research. 'Hello to Golden Goodbyes'. September 1993.
— 'Directorships Pay Rich Dividends'. October 1993.
— 'Tory Donations Another £1.6m'. January 1994.
— 'MPs Pay and Perks'.
— 'Keeping Shareholders Happy'. March 1994.
Audit Commission. *Minding the Quality*
— *Trusting in the Future.*
— *Their Health, Your Business: The New Role of the District Health Authority.*
National Audit Office Annual Report for 1993.

Books

Halloran, P. and Hollingsworth, M. *A Bit on the Side.* Simon & Schuster. 1994.
Matthew. H. C. G. *Gladstone.* Oxford University Press. 1986.
Riddle, P. *Honest Opportunism.* Hamish Hamilton. 1993.
Shannon, R. *Gladstone* Vol. I. Hamish Hamilton. 1981.

INDEX

INDEX

INDEX